D0057020

Churchill
A Very Peculiar History™

'The age of giants is over.'

Historian Sir Arthur Bryant
on the death of Sir Winston Churchill, 1965

For Beth,
my staunch Churchillian

DA

Editor: Nick Pierce

Artist: David Lyttleton
Additional artwork: Shutterstock

Published in Great Britain in MMXVIII by
Book House, an imprint of
The Salariya Book Company Ltd
25 Marlborough Place, Brighton BN1 1UB
www.salariya.com

ISBN: 978-1-912233-37-3

SALARIYA
SCRIBO   BOOK HOUSE   SCRIBBLERS

1 3 5 7 9 8 6 4 2

A CIP catalogue record for this book is available
from the British Library.

Printed and bound in China.
Printed on paper from sustainable sources.

Visit
www.salariya.com
for our online catalogue and
free fun stuff.

Churchill
A Very Peculiar History™

With added blood, toil,
tears and sweat

Written by
David Arscott

Created and designed by
David Salariya

BOOK HOUSE
a SALARIYA imprint

'You ask, what is our aim? I can answer
in one word: It is victory, victory at all
costs, victory in spite of all terror . . .
for without victory there is no survival.'
Churchill's first speech as Prime Minister,
1940

'Of all the talents bestowed upon
men, none is so precious as the gift
of oratory. He who enjoys it wields
a power more durable than that of a
great king.'
From an unpublished essay

'It was a nation and race dwelling all
round the globe that had the lion heart.
I had the luck to be called upon to give
the roar.'
On his role in the Second World War

'Yes – and now bugger off!'
*To his young grandson, on being asked
if he was the greatest man in the world*

Contents

❛He is a wonderful creature, with a curious schoolboy simplicity ... and what someone said of genius – "a zigzag of lightning in the brain".❜

TWO FINGERS AND A CIGAR

hat do the actors Richard Burton, Orson Welles, Timothy Spall, Albert Finney, Michael Gambon, Julian Fellowes, Brian Cox, Timothy West, Robert Hardy (nine times) and Gary Oldman have in common?

Yes, they've all padded up, put a fat cigar to their lips, affected a slight slur of speech and emitted a resonant growl to give over-the-top performances of Winston Churchill on screen.

In an age of political pygmies, this man bestrides the narrow world like a Colossus.

And, talking of Shakespeare, what do the Bard and this mixed bunch of worthies have in common: Charles Darwin, Isambard Kingdom Brunel, Elizabeth the First, Oliver Cromwell, Sir Isaac Newton, Lord Nelson, Sir Ernest Shackleton, John Lennon and Diana, Princess of Wales?

Answer: they all made it to the top ten of a 2002 BBC poll to find the greatest Briton of all time – and yet they all finished in the wake of the indomitable Winston Churchill.

How did this staggering adulation come about? Not for being a mere politician, of course, but because of his role as 'saviour of the nation', the man who (metaphorically) looked Hitler in the eye, clenched his fist and declared – in tones that still ring down the ages – that 'we shall never surrender'.

At his state funeral the dean of St Paul's Cathedral expressed the hope that 'the memory of his virtues and his achievements may remain as a part of our national heritage, inspiring generations to come to emulate his magnanimity and patriotic devotion'.

Today, more than fifty years later, that boiler-suited figure raising two fingers in a victory salute has become an icon. Any UK politician (of any party or gender) keen to promote a campaign of bravura, toughness and easy patriotism readily assumes a bulldog Churchillian style. Vainglorious perhaps, but they all want to bask in his glow.

Household god

The enduring desire of populist leaders to be associated with the Churchill myth was epitomised by Donald Trump within days of becoming US president in 2017.

A bust of Churchill (given on loan by then British Prime Minister Tony Blair) had been installed in the Oval Office by George W. Bush, but his succesor, Barack Obama, replaced it with a head of the civil rights leader Martin Luther King.

That wasn't good enough for Mr Trump. The original bust had been returned to the British embassy, but his staff dug out another one and he summoned the media to show that the great man had again been given due pride of place.

A good smoke

Well-wishers sent tens of thousands of cigars to Churchill during the Second World War. His chief benefactor was the New York businessman Samuel Kaplan, who bought up 5,000 large La Coronas from Havana in 1940, had the premier's name put on the bands and sent regular supplies. Churchill later thanked him for 'those wonderful cigars that have cheered my long path through the war' – adding that the bands were regarded as souvenirs 'and gladly accepted wherever I go'.

After the war a Cuban businessman, Antonio Giraudier, got in on the act, and Churchill became a devotee of the monster 16.5 cm (6½ in) Don Joaquin brand he sent – after successfully requesting that the original band have the image of a mafioso-like character (in fact the manufacturer himself) taken off.

The Cuban cigar that bears his name today is even larger, at 18 cm (7 in), although there's no evidence that Churchill ever smoked one.

And did he ever do much more than take a few puffs and nibble the end? You never see him pictured with a stub!

On the credit side

But he was, as we'll see, much more than a war leader. Here are just a few of the Churchillian virtues we'll explore later:

- Physical bravery, sometimes foolish
- Self-confidence, whether justified or not
- Writing skills which won him the Nobel Prize for Literature
- Artistic skills which saw his paintings hung in a Paris gallery
- Eloquence, with a rich gift of phrase-making

'He is a wonderful creature', said the (often critical) Liberal prime minister Lord Herbert Asquith, 'with a curious schoolboy simplicity ... and what someone said of genius – "a zigzag of lightning in the brain".'

One of his many biographers, the former Labour home secretary Roy Jenkins, summed up his style as a rumbustiously energetic government minister: 'His natural instinct was to shake any apple tree within reach and to get as much fruit off it as he possibly could.'

On the debit side

Asquith's 'wonderful creature' did, however, have his fair share of failings:

- **Self-centredness** in pursuit of his 'destiny'
- **Arrogance:** he always knew best
- **Recklessness,** both physical and political
- **Drink:** rather too much of it
- **Gambling:** an occasional vice
- **Eloquence,** so that it was hard to shut him up

It's not surprising that over the course of a long and often tempestuous career some pretty unkind things were said about him, though they were often combined with a reluctant admiration.

Here's the sharp-tongued socialist intellectual Beatrice Webb on first meeting the up-and-coming young politician at a dinner party: 'Restless, almost intolerably so, without capacity for sustained and unexcited labour, egotistical, bumptious, shallow-minded and reactionary, but with a certain personal magnetism, great pluck and some originality, not of intellect but of character.' Phew!

And here's an exasperated monarch, Edward VII, at about the same time: 'As for Mr Churchill, he is almost more of [a] cad in office than he was in opposition.' Ouch!

While still new to the House of Commons, he was so successful in stirring things up by being loquaciously rude to the major political figures of the day (even to those in his own party) that he found himself blackballed from the prestigious Hurlingham Club which he had wanted to join as a polo-playing member.

Lords a-leaping

Despite his background, Churchill wasn't always a champion of traditional values – and as Liberal home secretary in 1910 he called for the abolition of the House of Lords.

Condemning 'hereditary and aristocratic privilege', he suggested that the Lords be replaced by an upper chamber of only 150 members, a hundred of them elected by 'fifty great two-member constituencies'.

No chance. It was an idea ahead of its time – and remains so today.

Black dog

Arguably Churchill's biggest enemy was what he called his 'black dog' – the bouts of depression that, from his youth onwards, would lay him low, sometimes for months.

Another feature of his personality was an impressive and optimistic energy – 'He has a thousand ideas a day', US president, Franklin D. Roosevelt, once said, 'four of which are good' – some have diagnosed his condition as bipolar.

'Had he been a stable and equable man', the psychiatrist Anthony Storr has written, 'he could never have inspired the nation. In 1940, when all the odds were against Britain, a leader of sober judgment might well have concluded that we were finished.'

In 2006 the mental health charity Rethink commissioned a controversial 2.7 m (9 ft) statue of Churchill wearing a straightjacket. 'The message we want to portray', a spokesman explained, 'is that it is possible to recover from mental illness and overcome it and be successful – because Churchill is an example of someone who was able to do that.'

> 'I have taken more out of alcohol
> than it has taken out of me.'

Making enemies

Churchill could be a maddening opponent – vivacious, voluble, domineering and often wildly unpredictable. Here are a few of the people he managed to rub up the wrong way over the years.

Liberals and Conservatives
Yes, both parties, because he switched sides twice and wasn't always on the best of terms with the party he was currently supposed to be supporting. (This meant he was sometimes ignored even when talking good sense.)

Indians
A fervent believer in the British Empire, he opposed Indian self-rule, memorably describing Mahatma Gandhi, the leader of the independence movement, as 'a seditious Middle Temple lawyer, now posing as a fakir of a type well known in the East, striding half-naked up the steps of the Vice-regal palace'.

Suffragettes

Churchill was a qualified believer in women's suffrage, and had even voted for it, but when his support wavered and he declared provocatively 'I am not going to be henpecked on a question of such grave importance', the Suffragettes began to target his political meetings. One of them, the young Theresa Garnett, attacked him with a dogwhip.

Miners

He had a patrician fondness for the working man, but as home secretary in 1911 he had to deal with rioting that accompanied a miners' strike in the Rhondda, south Wales.

Clever clogs

Churchill had a genuine sympathy for the poor, but flinched at imagining how he might cope with the deprivations they suffered.

'Fancy living in one of these streets', he said to a friend as they walked through a poorer part of Manchester. 'Never seeing anything beautiful – never eating anything savoury – never saying anything clever!'

The local police had called in the military, but Churchill, whom *The Times* accused of weakness, held back all but a detachment of the Lancashire Fusiliers, and the harshest violence on the part of the authorities was meted out by police officers using rolled-up mackintoshes.

Thanks to his gung-ho reputation, however, a legend persists to this day that Winston Churchill ordered troops to open fire on the miners at Tonypandy.

Cometh the hour

Such was the man – brilliant, troubled, brave, irrepressible, opinionated, arrogant, admired, hated, flawed, endlessly gabbling – to whom a a desperate nation turned in 1940.

Until that moment he had, by his own lights, failed to meet the call of destiny. He had striven but had fallen short of the greatest prize.

It's a Very Peculiar Fact that, had the Second World War never chanced along, we would probably be looking back on his eventful life as a fascinating failure.

'the naughtiest
small boy in
the world '

CHAPTER ONE

A TARNISHED SPOON

You might imagine that a lad descended from the Duke of Marlborough and who first saw the light of day in the splendours of Blenheim Palace was born with the proverbial silver spoon in his mouth.

Not quite. Even his place of birth (a chilly bedroom in his grandfather's grand pile) was an accident: a swanky Mayfair pad had been kitted out for the event, but his mother had a fall while visiting Blenheim and her firstborn popped out two months early.

In fact, young Winnie's spoon was rather tarnished.

Blenheim Palace

Designed by John Vanbrugh in the English Baroque style, and now a UNESCO World Heritage Site, Blenheim Palace in Oxfordshire was originally a gift from the nation (along with the Woodstock Estate) to Charles Churchill, 1st Duke of Marlborough, for his military victories against the French and Bavarians, most famously at the Battle of Blenheim in 1704.

An ambitious soldier-statesman, Churchill was forced from office during political squabbles in the reign of Queen Anne and returned from self-imposed exile only after George I came to the throne some years later.

The palace had fallen into a poor state of repair by the time of Winston Churchill's birth, and the family into financial hardship, but in 1895 the 9th Duke (Winston's cousin) went through an arranged marriage with Consuelo, heiress of the immensely rich Vanderbilt railroad family, and the estate's future was assured.

Winston Churchill is buried not in the chapel at Blenheim Palace, but in the grounds of the nearby church of Bladon, alongside his parents.

Of course Churchill's family had rather more spare cash than the likes of us – but they were the sort of free-spending aristos who never seemed to have quite had enough of it and so were constantly running up large debts.*

On top of this, his parents were much too interested in their own affairs to pay much attention to young Winston. Not only was he packed off to a series of boarding schools (par for the course in those circles), but they wrote to him infrequently and paid him visits only when it was strictly necessary.

Distant Dad

Lord Randolph, his father, was a brightly flashing (and quickly fading) political comet whose career the young Winston sometimes seemed in danger of mimicking. A brilliant speaker, he was often rude to his superiors in parliament and so made unnecessary enemies.

---

* Churchill followed suit. As a young man he airily dismissed one of his mother's regular complaints about his spending: 'There is no doubt that we are both you and I equally thoughtless – spendthrift and extravagant.'

By the time Winston was 11 years old this charismatic, heavily moustachioed father had stirred parliament with his oratory, risen to Chancellor of the Exchequer in the Tory government and had a tactical (and extremely unwise) resignation readily accepted – so casting him for ever into the political wilderness. He was only 36, and he died nine years later.

The sad fact is that Lord Randolph had little time for a son who idolised him – who would later write a biography making him into a more significant figure than he really was; who named his own son after him; and who chose to be buried next to him – but who hardly knew him at all.

When he did make a rare appearance he was grouchy and discouraging, clearly thinking that the young Winston would never amount to much. Years later, after a convivial dinner with his own son, Churchill made the wistful comment, 'We have this evening had a longer period of continuous conversation together than the total which I ever had with my father in the whole course of his life.'

Missing mum

His mother was no better, though he thought the world of her, too. Born Jennie Jerome, she was the daughter of an American financial speculator and was clearly the impulsive type – she agreed to marry Randolph only three days after meeting him at a Cowes regatta party.

'She shone for me like the Evening Star', Churchill wrote later. 'I loved her dearly – but at a distance.'

Infant unisex

Victorians put their little lads in dresses until they were about six years old, when they were 'breeched' – that is, upgraded to trousers.

At Bexhill Museum in East Sussex you can see a cotton dress young Winston wore. Its ample dimensions suggest that he was a sturdy tot.

Parties were very much Jennie's thing – together with the amorous delights that went with them. Churchill's biographers have spent a good deal of printers' ink debating the parentage of his younger brother Jack, but the clear consensus is that he wasn't Randolph's boy.

Gossipy note: the Anglo-Irish novelist George Moore claimed that Lady Randolph had, somewhat heroically, two hundred lovers in all. Surely not!

Enter Woomany

Like many lads of his class, Churchill found alternative mothering in a beloved nurse. She was Mrs (a courtesy title, as she never married) Elizabeth Everest. He called her Woomany, and – in teenage letters to her – 'Darling Old Woom', a nickname she happily used herself in reply.

She remained with the family until Jack grew up, and it's a sign of her central place in his life that Churchill visited her several times during her last illness and was present at her deathbed.

'She had', he wrote, 'been my dearest and most intimate friend during the whole of the twenty years I had lived.'

He paid for her headstone in the City of London Cemetery and Crematorium at Newham and gave an annual sum to the local florist for the upkeep of the grave.

While Woomany would never have claimed to be anything other than a faithful family servant, however close, the Countess of Wilton was a regular fond correspondent who would address him as 'Dearest Winston' and sign off: 'With best love, Yr ever affecte. deputy mother, Laura Wilton.'

That was certainly putting Lady Randolph in her place . . .

A flogger's paradise

When he was just seven his parents sent him off to St George's school in Ascot, Berkshire – a financially well-endowed establishment which regarded itself as a mini Eton College but used the birch even more unsparingly.

'Two or three times a month', Churchill later recalled, 'the whole school was marshalled in the Library, and one or more delinquents were hauled off to an adjoining apartment by the two head boys, and there flogged until they bled freely, while the rest sat quaking, listening to their screams.'

It's not surprising that he failed to settle down in this educational bearpit. Here's his school report for April 1884:

Composition: Improved.
Grammar: Improved.
Diligence: Conduct has been exceedingly bad. He is not to be trusted to do any one thing. He has however notwithstanding made decided progress.
No. of times late: 20. Very disgraceful.
History/Geography: Very good, especially History.
Writing and spelling: Both very much improved.
Drawing: Fair, considering.
General conduct: Very bad. Is a constant trouble to everybody and is always in some scrape or other.
Headmaster's remarks: He cannot be trusted to behave himself anywhere. He has very good abilities.

Sussex by the sea

A few months later Churchill escaped, no doubt blessing a period of ill health which prompted the family doctor to prescribe his removal to the healthy sea air of Hove.

Here he entered a tiny (fewer than twenty pupils) and much more gentle establishment run by the Thomson sisters Kate and Charlotte. Although one of the mistresses declared, perhaps affectionately, that he was 'the naughtiest small boy in the world', he enjoyed his studies, got in a lot of swimming and learned to ride.

A bad hat

However justified in his criticism of the cruel punishments meted out at St George's, the headstrong young Winston often invited retribution.

On one occasion he stole sugar from the school pantry. On another he daringly entered the headmaster's study, ran off with his favourite straw hat and kicked it to pieces. *Courage!*

Insofar as he had any religious convictions at all they were borrowed from his Woomany, who was decidedly Low Church, and when the lads were taken to the Chapel Royal in Brighton for the Sunday service Winston stubbornly declined to turn to the east during the Creed, feeling it was a Popish thing to do.

A punishment was unnecessary: the following Sunday he found the school filing into pews that were already facing east!

Winnie scrape 1

Throughout his life Churchill put himself in the way of danger but always managed to come out alive, if sometimes a little worse for wear.

An incident during a drawing class at his Hove school was something of a trial run for future escapades. He made the mistake of tweaking another boy's ear, and his victim retaliated by sticking a penknife into his chest.

It had penetrated, Charlotte Thomson reassured his parents, a mere quarter of an inch – and the other boy had been expelled.

His health was still a problem. Towards the end of his stay in Hove he went down with a dose of double pneumonia – and his condition was considered so life-threatening that both of his parents managed to put their busy lives on hold and come down to visit him.

A Harrowing experience

They had 'put him down' for the prestigious Harrow School, and Charlotte Thomson accompanied him to London to take the entrance exam. It was touch and go, and – probably worried for her own reputation as much as for her young protégé – she was violently sick afterwards.

The worst part of it was that there were Latin and Greek translations, for which he had no aptitude at all (he later claimed to have left the Latin paper blank, save for his name), and no papers on his favourite subjects, English, history and geography. Somehow he squeezed through. Did his name help?

Now he was propelled into the educational big league – to sink or to swim.

In later life Churchill liked to give the impression that he had been a complete dunce at Harrow. It's true that he never mastered Latin and Greek, but he compensated for that failure by excelling at English.

His greatest feat was winning the Declamation Prize by faultlessly reciting from memory 1,200 lines of Macaulay's *Lays of Ancient Rome* – though the Classics scholars probably thought that was a complete waste of time.

What mattered most at a top people's school like Harrow was meeting the stars of the future and making an impression on them they wouldn't forget. That was something that Copperknob (as they called him for his reddish hair) was particularly good at.

The brash, impulsive young Winston got off to a mixed start in his first month by pushing an unsuspecting fellow pupil into the swimming pool, thinking (because of his small size) that he was someone of his own age. It turned out to be Leo Amery, a sixth former three years older, then head of house and champion at gym.

> 'They told me how Mr Gladstone
> read Homer for fun, which I thought
> served him right.'

Winston was, quite rightly, flung into the
deep end for his cheek, but the pair ended up
laughing and – he wrote in his entertaining
memoir *My Early Life* – 'we were afterwards to
be Cabinet colleagues for a good many years'.

Of course!

Winnie scrape 2

Strong swimmer though he was, Churchill
almost drowned while holidaying with a friend
at Lake Geneva in Lausanne.

The pair had jumped from their rowing boat
a mile from shore, only to see it being carried
away in the breeze – and 'now I saw Death as
near I believe I have ever seen him'.

Twice the boat moved away when he was within
yards of it until, exhausted, he managed to grab
it at the third attempt.

Churchill was no good at school ball games, but he represented his house at swimming and made a particular success of fencing. In 1889 he had written to his mother asking her to sub his involvement: 'I think it would be so much better for me to learn something which would be useful to me in the army, as well as affording me exercise and amusement.'

Three years later he won the public schools championship, telling her that it was 'a very fine cup. I was far and away first. Absolutely untouchable in the finals.'

What a modest lad!

It was three years before his father deigned to write to him – one of only five letters in all the years he was at Harrow – and that was in response to news that he would soon be taking exams to enter the school's army class.

Back in Winston's nursery days Lord Randolph had put his head round the door (a rare event) to find his son playing with his collection of 1,500 lead soldiers arranged in military formation. It gave him an idea.

'Winston never saw the
point of coming second'

Since the boy was so second-rate, Randolph thought, he would never make the bar or any profession requiring intellectual ability. Would he consider joining the army as a career? Yes, the innocent lad agreed – and so his fate was sealed.

Churchill duly passed into Harrow's army class, which prepared boys for entry into the elite Sandhurst officers' college, the Royal Military Academy, and when that time approached he was of course excited by the prospect. After all, he could easily see his way to achieving fame as a military commander. The only fly in the ointment was the passing of more of those wretched exams . . .

Captain James to the rescue

It was bad luck that Latin was part of the Sandhurst exam, but perhaps not surprising therefore that (to his father's fury) he failed it – not once, but twice.

The solution was to leave Harrow and enrol in a renowned London crammer ('Jimmies') run by Captain Walter James.

'It was said', Churchill wrote later, 'that no one who was not a congenital idiot could avoid passing thence into the Army' – and so, on the third attempt, he did.

It was, though, a lowly pass. Lord Randolph had earmarked his son for the infantry (he fancied the 60th Rifles), but Winston's marks fitted him 'only' for a cadetship in the cavalry.

Winnie scrape 3

While cramming for his third Sandhurst exam, the eighteen-year-old Churchill took a winter break at the Bournemouth estate of his aunt, Lady Wimborne.

Playing a game of chase with his young brother and a cousin, he found himself trapped on an ornamental bridge across a deep chine, his pursuers stationed at either end. The only possible way of escape was a leap into fir trees alongside the bridge – but his grasp failed and he fell 8.8 m (29 ft) to the ground beneath.

He was unconscious for three days, suffered a ruptured spleen, was attended by an army of eminent specialists and convalesced for a year.

Winston's grandmother, the Duchesss of Marlborough, was so pleased by his news that she promised to buy him a charger (a cavalryman's horse), but here's Lord Randolph's withering response in a letter he would rather *not* have received:

With all the advantages you had, with all the abilities which you foolishly think yourself to possess . . . with all the efforts that have been made to make your life easy & agreeable . . . this is the grand result that you come up among the 2nd rate and 3rd rate class who are only good for commissions in a cavalry regiment!

And beat this for the icing on the cake:

I am certain that if you cannot prevent yourself from leading the idle useless unprofitable life you have had during your schooldays & later months, you will become a mere social wastrel, one of the hundreds of public school failures, and you will degenerate into a shabby unhappy & futile existence.

That wounding criticism would have been enough to break most sensitive souls, but perhaps it helped to spur Winston on.

He was, in any event, delighted to be joining the cavalry with the horses he loved, and he simply couldn't wait to escape from those many largely fruitless years of schooling.

'At Sandhurst', he wrote, 'I had a new start. I was no longer handicapped by past neglect of Latin, French or Mathematics. We had now to learn fresh things and we all started equal.'

The life of the Winston Churchill history recognises was about to begin . . .

'Ambition was the
motive force and
he was powerless
to resist it. '

CHAPTER TWO

THE WARRIOR JOURNALIST

I t's a scarcely believable transformation, but the callow, rash, opinionated and academically tainted young man who both metaphorically and physically limped into the Sandhurst military academy in September 1893, and was commissioned a second lieutenant in the 4th Hussars eighteen months later, would become a nationally known figure before the century was out and while he was still no more than 25 years old.

Churchill had not only seized the opportunity to recast his life, but had done so using two weapons – the pen and the sword.

A lost watch

The strange tale of the valuable watch lost (and found) while he was at Sandhurst is revealing of both Churchill's determination and the fraught relationship with his father.

Lord Randolph had given him the Dent watch, complete with half-hunter case and the family coat of arms engraved and enamelled on the back. While leaning over the River Blackwater that ran through the college grounds, the horrified cadet saw it fall from his pocket into deep water.

After diving in without success, he paid for more than twenty of his fellow cadets to dig out a separate course for the river, then commandeered the Sandhurst fire engine to pump the spot dry.

By these desperate measures he retrieved the watch, and Churchill sent it off to Dent's for repair. By rotten luck Lord Randulph visited the shop soon after it arrived and discovered that his son had let him down yet again.

'When I get it back from Mr Dent', he wrote sternly, 'I shall not give it back to you.' True to his word, he sent a cheaper replacement.

Sandhurst itself was hard work but very much to Churchill's taste. He didn't much like the drill, and was for some months in the so-called 'Awkward Squad' of those who were deemed to need smartening up, but he threw himself into the practical effort of building trenches, blowing up masonry bridges, making maps and the like, and he amassed a library of books on military tactics.

At the end of the year's training he passed out with honours, ranked eighth out of a class of 150.

Galloping consumption

For a financially precarious family such as the Churchills a serious downside to joining a cavalry regiment was a young officer's costs in keeping up with his well-heeled colleagues in the mess. His pay covered less than a quarter of what he needed in the way of horses, uniform and other expenses.

Lord Randolph, to be fair, had quickly come round to his son's chosen path, but he died only weeks after seeing him join the Hussars.

It now fell to his mother to support the spendthrift young Winston. Where there had been a distance there was now – or so he described it in his memoirs – a relationship almost of partners: 'She was still at forty young, beautiful and fascinating. We worked together on equal terms, more like brother and sister than mother and son.'

But it was Lady Randolph who held the purse strings, and she wasn't much amused by her son's philosophy of raising cash to meet his needs rather than cutting back on his pleasures in order to fall in line with her bank balance.

Here's a typical rebuke: 'I went to Cox's this morning [Cox's & King's, army agents] & find out that not only have you anticipated the whole of your quarter's allowance due this month but £45 besides – & now this cheque for £50 – & that *you knew* you had nothing in the bank . . .'

You need to multiply those figures by about 50 for their equivalent today, so you can see why she was quite miffed about it.

And here's a typical response: 'We both know what is good and we both like to have it . . . I sympathise with all your extravagances – even more than you do with mine – it seems just as suicidal to me when you spend £200 on a ball dress as it does to you when I purchase a new polo pony for £100.

'And yet I feel that you ought to have the dress and I the polo pony. The pinch of the whole matter is that we are damned poor.'

fun in Cuba

It's hard to imagine in our war-torn times, but a restless young soldier at the end of the nineteenth century could fear that he'd never get to experience any thrilling enemy action.

That's certainly how Churchill saw it. He was envious of the grizzled veterans in the ranks who had come under fire in those distant, heady days before the world 'languished' – what a loaded word he used! – in a seemingly endless peace.

He thought it was time for an adventure.

Perhaps it was because of such a long peace that the military 'season' in Britain was only seven months long. That meant soldiers had a five-month winter break from their duties – and Churchill and his fellow subaltern Reginald Barnes decided to use it by getting some first-hand experience of danger.

Cuba was still under colonial rule at that time, and the Spanish army was attempting to suppress rebels in the jungle. Off the pair went, after arranging the suitable permissions, and they were soon trotting alongside General Suarez Valdez – not as combatants, but allowed to use their weapons in self defence.

Churchill got a little of what he wanted, coming under fire for the very first time on his 21st birthday, but his later account of the episode is droll to the point of comic. Engagements between the two sides were sporadic and neither could hope to win: 'We withdrew across the plain to La Jicotea. Spanish honour and our own curiosity alike being satisfied, the column returned to the coast, and we to England.'

A passage to India

The 4th Hussars sailed for India in October 1896, giving the young officer his first foreign posting. The regiment would remain on the sub-continent for more than a dozen years – but don't imagine that the young Churchill meant to hang around with them for long.

Winnie scrape 4

It took no time at all for Churchill to suffer his first misadventure in India. His troopship having cast anchor in Bombay Harbour, he and two other officers climbed into a skiff to take them ashore ahead of the main disembarkment. The little vessel pitched wildly in the swell as it approached a stone wall with dripping steps and iron rings for handholds.

Having reached out for one of these rings, he was tugged viciously backwards by the tossing boat and his shoulder was all but wrenched out of its socket. It wasn't a complete dislocation, but the injury dogged Churchill all his life – and when he played polo he had to have his arm strapped up.

Churchill was a young man in a hurry. Thanks to his pedigree, and in particular to his father's career, he had an easy entry into the world of politics in which he meant to make his mark. His military career was merely a stepping-stone on the way to the top.

The life of a subaltern in Bangalore, where the Hussars were based, seems to have been pretty cushy – servants to wait on him, a groom for his horses, a comfortable bungalow to live in, an endless round of polo matches, regular home leave – but it couldn't satisfy our thrusting young man.

After all, there was no fighting going on.

Here's his hectic itinerary in the 18 months after arriving in India:

- **A great start: Winnie's polo team wins the Golconda Cup in Hyderabad.**

- **He hears that there's fighting against Pathan tribesmen on the Indian frontier and gets leave from his regiment to join the Malakand Field Force under Major General Sir Bindon Blood.**

- Is commissioned as a war correspondent by the Indian paper the *Pioneer*, with simultaneous publication in the *Daily Telegraph*.

- Having travelled an exhausting 3,200 km (about 2,000 miles) to get there at his own expense, he sees action in the Mamund Valley, exchanges fire with the enemy and helps rescue an injured officer.

- As an emergency he's posted as an officer to the 31st Punjab Infantry, which has only its colonel and three white officers left. His journalism (anonymous letters 'From a Young Officer') is well received.

- Recalled to Bangalore, he agitates to return to the frontier. Thwarted, he instead writes his first book, *The Malakand Field Force* – and receives a complimentary letter about it from the future Edward VII.

- The Hussars reach the semi-finals of the Cavalry Cup, but lose to the Durham Light Infantry.

- Manages to get back to the frontier again – only to find that the fighting has ended.

Not quite fiction

Somehow, during this period of hectic travel, a little fighting, his journalism and the Malakand book, Churchill managed to write a novel which was serialised in *Macmillan's Magazine* from May to December 1899.

Savrola is a wooden, beginner's attempt at fiction, with Churchill's own family and circle featuring in only thin disguise. The dazzling heroine Lucile, surely his mother ('foreign princes had paid her homage, not only as the loveliest woman in Europe...') is married to the ineffectual Balkan ruler/Lord Randolph ('...a look of awful weariness, as of one who toils and yet foresees that his labour will be in vain'.)

Enter – we blush at the Freudian implications – the bold hero Savrola, otherwise Churchill himself, a man raised by a wise and faithful nurse, a man whose cast of mind is 'vehement, high and daring' and who makes off with the infatuated Lucile.

'Ambition was the motive force', we read, 'and he was powerless to resist it.'

We rest our case.

Churchill's restless ambition, his obstinacy and his ability to rub people up the wrong way is epitomised by his attempt to be posted to the Sudan, where the British were striving to reconquer land the Mahdi had taken thirteen years before (when General Gordon was killed at Khartoum).

The man who stood in his way was the sirdar, or commander, of the Egyptian Army, Sir Herbert Kitchener – he of the 'Your Country Needs You' poster in the First World War.

Kitchener was aware that Churchill was energetically twisting influential arms in his well-connected circles (even the prime minister spoke up for him), but he evidently regarded the young officer as an uncouth upstart eager for medals and publicity.

Churchill was equally scathing: 'He may be a general,' he wrote, 'but never a gentleman.'

And who won? At the end of July 1898 the young subaltern joined a boat in Marseilles, a contract from the *Morning Post* in his pocket, to join the 21st Lancers in Cairo.

There was, though, one important proviso. The War Office wrote to him: 'It is understood that you will proceed at your own expense and that in the event of your being killed or wounded in the impending operations, or for any other reason, no charge of any kind will fall on British Army funds.'

A last hurrah

Churchill was in the Sudan for only two months, but of course he saw some exciting action, enhanced his reputation for bravery and got out of it not only newspaper articles but material for another book he was writing.

The action was the famous Battle of Omdurman, one of the last cavalry charges by the British Army. Like the equally famous Charge of the Light Brigade in the Crimea a generation earlier, it was far less glorious than its reputation suggests.

By a turn of events he must have relished, Churchill was the officer chosen by a colonel at the front line to ride back to Kitchener himself and urge immediate reinforcements.

'You have got at least an hour,' he reported, 'probably an hour and a half, sir, even if they come on at their present rate.'

As Churchill later recorded it, 'He tossed his head in a way that left me in doubt whether he accepted or rejected this estimate, and then with a slight bow signified that my mission was discharged.'

The 21st Lancers lost 21 men in the battle, roughly the same number as the 'whirling Dervishes' they attacked, while 50 were wounded and 119 horses destroyed.

Don't mind if I do ...

On the eve of the Battle of Omdurman Churchill was strolling by the Nile when the junior naval lieutenant David Beatty (later to be Britain's longest-ever serving First Sea Lord) tossed him a magnum of champagne from a gunboat.

It fell short, but Churchill – never one to refuse a drink – happily waded in up to his knees to retrieve it.

Churchill himself emerged unscathed and, using a Mauser automatic pistol rather than a sword because of his injured shoulder, claimed to have killed several of the enemy: '3 for certain – 2 doubtful.'

His book of the campaign, published in 1899, was *The River War*, an impressive two-volume work subtitled *An Historical Account of the Reconquest of the Soudan*. In the section on Omdurman he fired off a few volleys at Kitchener, for ordering the shooting of injured dervishes on the field of battle and for later descecrating the Mahdi's tomb: Kitchener with great callousness, turned his skull into an inkwell.

Soldier's farewell

As the century drew to a close Churchill decided that it was time to quit soldiering. It had served its purpose in winning him notoriety as a man brave under fire, but 'Her Majesty was so stinted by Parliament', he later wrote waggishly, 'that she was not able to pay me even a living wage'. He had proved that he could earn more from his pen.

And then there was politics, to which he was increasingly drawn. He began to sound out the chances of winning a seat in parliament.

First, though, there was to be one last attention-grabbing overseas adventure.

Winnie scrape 5

Churchill had one last assignment before leaving the Hussars – to take part in the inter-regimental polo tournament in Meerut, Uttar Pradesh. The officers of the 4th clubbed together to send 30 ponies on the 2,250 km (1,400 mile) journey in a special train.

One evening before the tournament he was invited to supper at the governor's residence by his old chief Sir Bindon Blood. The amount of drink taken over their reminiscences isn't recorded, but Churchill contrived to fall down the stairs, spraining both ankles and sustaining various bruises.

Together with his gippy shoulder, that was enough for him to offer standing down from the team. His comrades wouldn't hear of it, however – and they went on to a thrilling victory over the 2nd Dragoons in the final.

An engine of disaster

On the day he boarded the *Dunottar Castle* cruise liner bound for South Africa and the Boer War in October 1899 Churchill was one hundred per cent a journalist.* He had adroitly played the *Daily Mail* and the *Morning Post* against one another in order to secure a lucrative four-month contract from the *Post*.

By the time he descended the gangplank at Cape Town at the end of the month, however, his position had become more complicated. On board the ship he had met the colonel of the Lancashire Hussars, Lord Gerard, and drawn from him the promise of being commissioned in that yeomanry regiment once they arrived at the front.

Playing the dual role of writer and soldier wasn't new to him, of course – but this time it was to land him in deep trouble.

---

* His liquid supplies on board amounted to 60 bottles of champagne, claret, port, vermouth, brandy and whisky – plus lime juice. On the downside, he did suffer from bad sea-sickness.

> 'I play for high stakes and – given an audience – there is no act too daring or too noble.'

Churchill soon ran into an old acquaintance, Captain Aylmer Haldane, who had been detailed to reconnoitre the landscape with an armoured train and six trucks; a gun manned by six sailors; two small companies of fusiliers and infantrymen; and a breakdown gang.

It was a caper he simply couldn't resist!

Churchill, who was 'eager for trouble', very soon found it. They had gone no more than 22.5 km (14 miles) when they saw enemy forces on a hill behind them, and Haldane decided they had better retreat quickly to avoid being cut off from their base. As the train gathered speed downhill it was struck by shrapnel and spattered by bullets.

A nasty surprise lay in store: the Boers had sabotaged the track. There was a large crashing sound as the leading three trucks were thrown off their rails.

Churchill was now in his element – a situation of immense hopelessness and danger. He began to give orders.

The engine was still on its tracks, but it had been at the centre of the train with the three damaged trucks in front of it. The first had completely toppled over, killing and injuring members of the plate-laying team. The next two trucks, with the Durham Light Infantry on board, had been derailed, one lying on its side, and they were blocking the line. Haldane's Dublin Fusiliers were in the undamaged rear two trucks, with the naval gun behind. Meanwhile the Boers had gathered in their hundreds and were peppering the train with shells and artillery fire.

For more than an hour, while Haldane's men gave what cover they could against the whistling bullets and while the naval blue jackets fired salvoes from their seven-pounder, Churchill organised the shunting of the engine back and forth, time and again, until the heavy crippled trucks were pushed away from the track.

With the viciousness of the Boers' attack allowing no time to couple the remaining trucks to the engine, he got all the wounded aboard (some 40 in all) and ordered the driver to cross a nearby bridge and wait for the remaining troops on the other side.

He then jumped off the train to return to Haldane – and that was a big mistake . . .

Just desserts

Charles Wagner, the engine driver, was dazed and injured in the derailment and was apparently reluctant to put his (civilian) life in further danger. Churchill knew they were lost without him, 'so I told him that no man was hit twice on the same day: that a wounded man who continued to do his duty was always rewarded for distinguished gallantry, and that he might never have this chance again'.

No reward was forthcoming, but Churchill was able to put that right ten years later when he was home secretary. He checked the railway company records and recommended Wagner and his fireman for the Albert medal, the highest civilian award for gallantry.

Unknown to him, Haldane's small force had been surrounded and captured. Walking along the tracks Churchill was confronted by two enemy riflemen about 90 m (100 yards) off. He dashed away and scrambled up a bank as their bullets flew about him ('Two soft kisses sucked in the air'), but just when he thought himself out of range a rifleman on horseback appeared before him. Churchill reached for his pistol, but he had left it aboard the train in all the confusion. He surrendered.

At the Boer headquarters he was separated from the captured fusiliers and feared the worst: 'I had enough military law to know that a civilian in half uniform who has taken an active and prominent part in a fight, even if he has not fired a shot himself, is liable to be shot at once by a drumhead court-martial.'

He was, as usual, in luck. 'We aren't going to let you go, old chappie', one of his captors quipped. 'We don't catch the son of a lord every day.' He was reunited with Haldane and his men to be route-marched about 100 km (60 miles) and put on a train to Pretoria as a prisoner of war in a converted school building.

What *was* his status? As far as Churchill was concerned his chance of getting out depended on it

- Shortly after being captured he applied for his release on the grounds that he was a non-combatant: 'I have consistently adhered to my character as a press representative, taking no part in the defence of the armoured train and being quite unarmed.'

- Days later, having heard that there was a prisoner exchange in the air, he asked the assistant adjutant-general in the War Office to classify him a military officer.

A deal was indeed in the offing, but Churchill was simply too impatient to wait.

The great escape

On the night of 12 December he scaled a wall, dropped to freedom and set off on a perilous 450 km (280-mile) journey to Portuguese Mozambique. He spoke no Afrikaans or Kaffir and, because of his notoriety, would soon have a large price on his head.

A bit of a chancer

It's typical of the headstrong young Churchill that his bold prison escape brought him scathing criticism for his opportunism as much as admiration for his courage.

He had made the South African government promises about his conduct if they let him go (including a return to Europe), and the Boer commander growled that he had broken the terms of his parole – although, of course, no deal had yet been agreed.

A more serious accusation was made by Haldane. Years later, now a distinguished general, he still harboured bitter feelings about that solo dash for freedom. He, Churchill and a Sergeant Major Brockie had originally planned to escape together.

'I was surprised and disgusted to find myself left in the lurch', he wrote, 'for Churchill had walked off with my carefully thought-out plan or what he knew of it, and had simply taken the bread out of my mouth.'

Churchill claimed it was a misunderstanding, but it's pretty clear that he had once again been ruled by his habitual impulsiveness.

Churchill (of course) later wrote up the tale of his adventure, displaying a gift for telling detail and imbuing his time on the run with the excitement of a *Boys' Own* story.

Wearing a brown flannel civilian suit, and with a few biscuits and a large wad of money in his pockets, he walked alongside a railway line in the darkness, eventually leaping aboard a goods train and hiding himself under a pile of coal sacks.

Some hours later, before daylight, he jumped down beside the track and took shelter in a wood, knowing that he must travel only under cover of darkness. On the second night, feeling increasingly desperate, he came upon the lights of a coal mine and decided to take the risk of banging his fist on a door.

It was opened (more Churchill luck) by an Englishman – John Howard, manager of the Transvaal Collieries – who told him 'Thank God you have come here! It's the only house for 32 km (20 miles) where you would not have been handed over. We are all British here, and we will see you through.'

While Howard hatched a plan to spirit him away there was only one safe place to hide. Churchill was taken into the mine and introduced to Dan Dewsnap of Oldham, 'who locked my hand in a grip of crushing vigour', opened the door to the cage and dropped the three of them down into 'the bowels of the earth'. They followed a labyrinth of tunnels to a chamber where two Scottish miners carrying lanterns were waiting with a mattress and blankets.

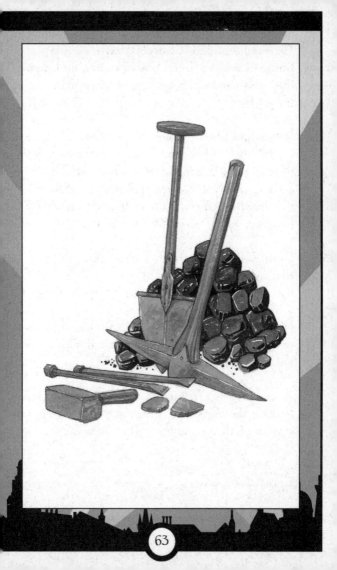

Howard handed Churchill two candles, a bottle of whisky and a box of cigars, and then they wished him goodnight and returned to the surface.

When he woke the following morning, he was unable to find his candles, so patiently waited in the pitch darkness. Howard – eventually arriving with food – explained that, as he hadn't thought to stuff them under his mattress, they had been eaten by rats.*

Churchill spent another day and night in the pit and was eventually smuggled on to a train bound for Mozambique. Supplied with a revolver, two roast chickens, a few slices of meat, a loaf of bread, a melon and three bottles of cold tea, he hid in a goods truck among large bales of wool.

At last, peering through a gap in the planking, he saw the caps of Portuguese officials on a station platform and knew that he was safe.

* 'I saw numbers of rats', he later wrote. 'They seemed rather nice little beasts, quite white, with dark eyes which I was assured in the daylight were a bright pink.'

'As we rumbled and banged along, I pushed my head out of the tarpaulin and sang and shouted and crowed at the top of my voice. Indeed, I was so carried away by thankfulness and delight that I fired my revolver in the air two or three times as a *feu de joie*.'

No one has disputed the grit and daring of his nail-biting escapade, but just as General Haldane disputed the way it began, so it later came to light that a local merchant, Charles Burnham – shipper of those wool bales – had prevented a search of his truck on the journey into Mozambique by travelling on the train and paying bribes to any officials bent on carrying out an inspection.

World famous overnight

It was his son Randolph who coined the phrase in his biography of Churchill. After checking in to the British consulate in Lourenço Marques (today's Maputo), the dashing escapee took a boat to Durban, arriving two days before Christmas 1899 to discover that he was 'world famous overnight'.

In Durban he received 'sheaves of telegrams' from wellwishers around the world, the harbour was bedecked with flags, bands played, and he stood before a large crowd outside the town hall 'where nothing would content them but a speech, which after a becoming reluctance I was induced to deliver'.

That was tongue-in-cheek modesty, of course. Winston Churchill was now a star, and he was very happily aware of the fact.

Cash in hand

John Howard, the mine manager, took a great risk in helping Churchill, and his son claimed that after his role eventually came to light a Boer commandant and five burghers arrived to arrest him.

Howard treated them to glasses of whisky, equipped himself with two loaded pistols and then – prepared to bring the matter to a bloody conclusion if necessary – offered them cash if they would let him go.

Yes, a juicy bribe worked once again.

What it meant was that he was now perfectly set up for the next stage in his burgeoning career.

First, it's true, there was a little more war reporting/semi-detached soldiering to do. He was present at the bloodbath of Spion Kop and at the Relief of Mafeking as the Boer War drew to a close. He even achieved the daring feat of cycling through the centre of Johannesburg in civilian clothes to take an important message to General Roberts while the city was still (weakly) occupied by the Boers.

There were also books to see through the press: between 1898 and 1900 he published no fewer than five on military themes.

But his heart was now set on entering the political arena – and, thanks to his reputation as a dashing national hero, he was simply unstoppable . . .

' In the twinkling
of an eye I found
myself without an
office, without a seat,
without a party and
without an appendix. '

CHAPTER THREE

POLITICAL MAVERICK

itching for one of the two Oldham seats during the 1900 general election, Churchill entered the town in triumph ('a procession of ten landaus'), regaled a crowd in the Theatre Royal with the story of his great escape from the Boers and praised the local engineer, Dan Dewsnap, for helping to shelter him down the mine.

At this a great cry went up: 'His [Dewsnap's] wife's in the gallery!'

Churchill had hit the jackpot again. With that kind of luck, he surely couldn't lose!

Catching up

The Winston Churchill who entered parliament when still a little short of his 26th birthday was keenly aware that he lacked the university education most of his peers had enjoyed.

He had, though, been attempting to make good this deficiency ever since joining the Hussars. In 1896 he began to build up a substantial library, with Lady Randolph posting out to India books ranging from history and philosophy to Darwin's *On The Origin of Species*, Adam Smith's *Wealth of Nations*, Plato's *Republic* and (surely a bit of a slog) the 27 volumes of the *Annual Register*, the record of major parliamentary debates and legislative developments.

What he did with these dry tomes was make a summary of each report he read, outline what his own response would have been and decide what he would have said and how he would have voted.

And that old bugbear, Latin? He'd gone so far as to learn some useful phrases, but Asquith would, he said later, flinch to hear him mispronounce them at Cabinet meetings.

He didn't, although it was a close-run thing. This was 'the khaki election', Churchill and his fellow Tories banking on the nation's thanks for having (almost) won the Boer War. Neville Chamberlain, the prime minister, put it starkly: 'Every seat lost to the government is a seat gained to the Boers.'

Churchill had, during a brief lull in his other activities, fought and lost a by-election in Oldham the year before. Enough Liberal voters now gave him the nod because of his war record for him to sneak into second place, and that was enough – by the rules of the time, the top two were elected.

So began the political career of a man controversial from the beginning, often unpredictable, never a party hack– ever the maverick.

Banking his reputation

Newcomer though he was to parliament, Churchill had something important to do before taking his seat in the House. MPs weren't paid in those days, and he badly needed to raise a large pot of cash.

What followed was a prodigious lecture tour, complete with magic lantern, in which he visited every major British city and made the most of his Boer escape story.

For five weeks he spoke practically every night except for Sunday, and when that was done he crossed the Atlantic and did the same for two months in the United States and Canada.

In the USA he met the soon-to-be president Theodore Roosevelt, who didn't take to him then or later (they were too alike, his sister thought), and the writer Mark Twain, who took issue with Churchill's nationalistic views.

By the time he decided to grace parliament with his presence for his maiden speech in February 1901 the elderly Queen Victoria had died, the crown passing to her son, Edward VII, and Churchill was, in today's terms, about a quarter of a million pounds better off than when he stepped ashore from his South African adventures. That little haul would keep him going for several years.

Opening remarks

Churchill, wearing a full-length frock coat, delivered his maiden speech by heart.

A reporter in the *Daily News* compared him with Lord Randolph*: 'Mr Churchill does not inherit his father's voice – save for the slight lisp – or his father's manner. Address, accent, appearance do not help him.

'But he has one quality – intellect. He has an eye – and he can judge and think for himself.'

The speech, not surprisingly, was on the war, and already an independent note suggested that he would before long be clashing with his Tory colleagues.

'If I were a Boer fighting in the field', he said. 'And if I were a Boer I hope I *should* be fighting in the field . . .'

* Meanwhile Winston had a new step-father. In July 1900 Lady Randolph married George Cornwallis-West – a Scots Guards officer who was just two weeks older than her son.

Churchill was always open to charges of jingoism for his fierce prosecution of any war he believed in, but also suspected of weakness when he declared that a defeated enemy deserved respect. Now he spoke out against the installation of an interim military rather than civilian government in South Africa.

'I have often myself been very much ashamed', he went on, 'to see respectable old Boer farmers... ordered about peremptorily by young subaltern officers as if they were private soldiers.'

free trade and all that

But his fiercest clash with his own party was over Free Trade. The Conservatives were moving towards a 'protectionist' policy, putting up tariffs to safeguard industry from foreign competition and making the British Empire a single trading bloc.

For Churchill, that meant higher food prices, to the benefit of big business and the well-off and to the detriment of the ordinary man and woman.

'No-one seems to care anything but about money today', he told a large meeting in Glasgow. 'Nothing is held of account except the bank accounts.'

And listen to this for left wingery: 'Quality, education, civil distinction, public virtue seem each year to be valued less and less. Riches unadorned seem each year to be valued more and more.'

Absent member

Churchill had better things to do than pay regular visits to his Oldham constituency, but the Conservative agent kept him up to date with conditions in the party's office.

'There is neither warmth nor comfort in the place', he wrote in December 1903. 'Through the recent frost one of my clerks is dead (pneumonia) and the other has acute bronchitis, & the two illnesses can only be attributed to the absence of any fire or warmth in the office, and to general damp, dark, unsanitary conditions.'

Four days later the other one died.

He who hesitates ...

In April 1904, while making a speech in the Commons, Churchill suffered one of the most traumatic moments of his public life – his famous memory let him down.

Perhaps it was the stress of again being in opposition to his own party's policy. He was on his feet to argue in favour of trades union rights and against the notorious Taff Vale court ruling which allowed unions to be sued for damages if they went on strike.

He had already been speaking for 45 minutes without notes when he completely dried up. Unable to go, he sat down with his head in his hands, clearly devastated. The Commons, mercifully, murmured in sympathy rather than howled with derision.

For a while after this he turned to Pelmanism, then a newly promoted system for improving mental faculties, now better known as a card game which relies on players' memories.

His lasting strategy was more mundane: he afterwards always arrived with a detailed and fool-proof set of notes.

> 'In the course of my life I have often had to eat my words, and I must confess that I have always found it a wholesome diet.'

During one of his House of Commons speeches his own prime minister walked out on him, followed by the rest of the Tory flock, so it wasn't a great surprise to anyone when in 1904, only four years after being elected, he switched sides to sit on the Liberal benches.

Liberal lion

During his twenty years with the Liberals Churchill had plenty of ups and downs, as we'll see, but also a clutch of ministerial posts:

- 1908 President of the Board of Trade: at 33 he's the youngest cabinet minister since 1866
- 1910 Home Secretary
- 1911 First Lord of the Admiralty
- 1917 Minister of Munitions
- 1918 War and Air Secretary
- 1921 Colonial Secretary

Enter Clemmie

One evening in March 1908 Churchill was invited to a London dinner and found himself seated next to a young woman he had first set eyes on four years earlier but had apparently not given a thought to since. She was Clemence Hozier – tall, attractive, somewhat reticent and almost a dozen years younger.

His romances until then seem to have been fitful and fairly tepid. Hers had been more advanced, since she had been engaged three times, twice (secretly) to the same man.

On this occasion he certainly took notice, and the feeling was evidently mutual. Within six months they were married.

For a contemporary view of the match we can't resist turning to a letter from Violet Asquith, the Liberal prime minister's daughter. She was a friend of Clemmie's, but since she always seemed to carry a torch for Winston it's only fair to point out that her barbed comments shouldn't be taken at face value.

'The news of the clinching of Winston's engagement to the Hozier has just reached me from him. I must say I am much gladder for her sake than I am sorry for his. His wife could never be more to him than an ornamental sideboard as I have often said and she is unexacting enough not to mind not being more. Whether he will ultimately mind her being as stupid as an *owl* I don't know... Father thinks that it spells disaster for them both.'

Clemmie was far from stupid, and she was certainly not content to be her husband's 'sideboard'. Throughout his long and turbulent political life she was time and again the quiet voice of reason, not afraid to point out where he was overstepping the mark – though knowing she would often be ignored.

It was in obvious ways a better deal for the self-centred Churchill, who needed endless cosseting, but despite Clemmie's occasional rages about his behaviour, Asquith's prediction of disaster was wide of the mark. He often pushed their marriage to its limits, but she made it work.

Oh, and you'd probably like to know that in their fonder notes to one another he gave her the nickname Kat while she called him Pig.*

Siege mentality

Churchill had a bit of a rocky time as home secretary. We've already seen that he made the miners and the suffragettes pretty angry, but ridicule was probably harder to take.

That was the outcome of the so-called Siege of Sidney Street. Two members of a Latvian terrorist gang who been caught trying to tunnel into a jeweller's shop, and had killed two policemen in their escape, were now holed up in a house in London's East End.

Having agreed that an armed platoon of Scots Guards from the Tower of London should join the police outside the house, Churchill couldn't resist going to the scene himself.

* *Tailor and Cutter* magazine unkindly described Churchill's clobber on the big day as 'one of the greatest failures as a wedding garment we have ever seen, giving the wearer a sort of glorified coachman appearance'.

After all, hadn't he very often ridden into danger on horseback (and even on a bicycle), and wasn't he used to being the centre of attention in dramatic situations which demanded his charismatic presence?

As tension mounted, there he stood in an astrakhan-collared overcoat, a top hat on his head, inevitably the centre of attention.

Changing seats

Churchill wasn't an Oldham MP for long. There was a general election in 1906, soon after he had switched parties, and he won the Manchester North seat for the Liberals.

His stay there was even shorter. By a law of the time new government ministers had to be re-elected by their constituences. He duly stood in Manchester after joining the Cabinet in 1908 – and the voters threw him out.

Never mind: there was always a place for such a bright up-and-coming young man. The Liberals found him a fairly safe berth in Dundee, and he was immediately back in parliament once again.

There was a grim gun battle. Another policeman was shot dead, the house burned down (with two charred bodies inside) and a fireman was killed by falling debris.

The home secretary's role was quickly called into question. He had probably given no operational orders to the police, though he did instruct the fire brigade to let the house burn down. But why was he there at all?

The Conservative leader Arthur Balfour had great fun at his expense in parliament. Both he and a photographer who snapped him at the scene were, he said, to hoots of laughter, risking valuable lives: 'I understand what the photographer was doing, but what was the honourable gentleman doing?'

Meanwhile a Pathé News film of the siege was showing in local cinemas – and when Churchill's face appeared some members of the audience called out 'Shoot him!'

Churchill later regretted 'a strong sense of curiosity which perhaps it would have been well to keep in check'.

"Dear King ..."

A special duty of the home secretary during Churchill's twenty months in the post was to write a nightly parliamentary letter to the king (first Edward VII and then, after his death in 1910, George V), reflecting on the previous day's parliamentary business.

A simple summary of events would no doubt have sufficed, but Churchill couldn't resist writing reams (by hand) and giving the monarch the benefit of his sage comments and occasional witty asides.

He went too far for the sensitive King George when commenting on a 'right to work' debate. After reporting that labour colonies were being considered for tramps and vagrants, he added the line: 'It must not however be forgotten that there are idlers and wastrels at both ends of the social scale.'

Shock, horror! Churchill was rapped over the knuckles in a letter from the palace which told him 'The King thinks that Mr Churchill's views ... are very socialistic.'

Churchill replied directly to George in a letter that was polite, but far from contrite.

Ruler of the King's navy

Moving from the Home Office to become First Lord of the Admiralty, as Churchill did in 1911, might have been regarded by some of his colleagues as a slight demotion, but it was a post he had long coveted.

Suddenly the boy who had played in his nursery with 1,500 lead soldiers was a man in charge of a huge real-life force with global pretensions, even if they were to be deployed on the sea, rather than land.

He also got to travel around on the lavishly provisioned Admiralty yacht, a 4.064-tonne (4,000 ton) craft with a crew of around two hundred. Despite a tendency to sea-sickness, that was just the kind of luxury he loved. He even used it (did nobody raise an eyebrow?) to take friends on sightseeing holidays.

Added to that, he had a mission. Many disagreed with him, but he could see a war on the horizon, and he felt that the country – and in particular the navy – wasn't properly prepared for it.

Here are a few of his achievements before that war duly arrived:

- He boldly got rid of several men at the top, including the First Sea Lord, in order to promote men he thought would do a better job.

- Having inherited an annual naval budget of £39 million, he talked this up until he was given more than £50 million, and he used the increase in part to build several more dreadnought battleships.

- He replaced the existing 34 cm (13½ in) battleship gun with one of 38.1 cm (15 in), so increasing explosive power by almost a third.

- He began the fleet's conversion from coal to oil, significantly increasing battleship speeds.

- He secured an improvement in lower-deck pay and conditions, to improve morale in the service.

Much of this was controversial, which meant that if things went wrong he wouldn't have many friends to defend him. And things very soon *did* go wrong . . .

When the First World War was declared, he was at first almost ecstatic, and rather guiltily so. 'Everything tends towards catastrophe and collapse', he wrote to Clemmie. 'I am interested, geared up and happy. Is it not horrible to be made like this?'

And then things didn't just go wrong – first they went pretty seriously wrong and then they turned disastrous.

What's in a name?

Shortly before the Great War, Charles Nevill, a go-getting developer, bought up a swathe of clifftop downland to the east of Brighton in Sussex and began to sell off plots of land to create a kind of Wild West shanty town with sea views.

During the war, Nevill decided to call his settlement New Anzac on Sea in honour of the Australian and New Zealand forces who were fighting alongside British and Allied troops.

After the bloodletting of Gallipoli he scrapped that idea and launched a national competition for a new name. Today it's Peacehaven.

Twerpish

First there was Antwerp. With the Belgian city under siege by the Germans from 28th September 1914 and on the point of evacuation, Churchill forgot all about Sidney Street (see pages 80-81) and decided that the best thing for everyone was for him to be in the thick of the action. ('Winston's sense of proportion deserted him', Clemmie would later say.)

Off he went to instil some backbone into the natives, even requesting that he be allowed to resign as First Lord and be made military commander of Antwerp – and the day after he got back, the city surrendered. The general view was that he was barmy.

Gallipoli

Next, and dreadfully, came the horror of Gallipoli for which Churchill took most of the blame. The war was only nine months old when combined Allied troops attempted to take control of the Dardanelles, the narrow strait dividing the Asian landmass of Turkey from Europe.

With troops bogged down in trench warfare on the Western Front, the bright idea was to attack the enemy from the east. But it wasn't really so bright: in many months of fierce fighting on the Gallipoli peninsula the Allied forces and their Ottoman opponents each lost more than 50,000 lives, with many more injured or missing, and neither could claim a clear victory.

Churchill's mistake, it was widely held, was to attempt a naval victory without sufficient land-army back-up. Asquith, in charge of a coalition government, promptly fired him and demoted him to Chancellor of the Duchy of Lancaster – a token job with the main duty of appointing magistrates for the county of Lancashire.

Having sent a desperate flurry of letters hoping to persuade Asquith to keep him on at the Admiralty, he finally succumbed: 'All right, I accept your decision. I shall not look back.'

Clemmie again: 'I thought he would die of grief.'

Trench warfare

What Churchill did next was remarkable even by his own standards. Still an MP, still firing off pronouncements to all and sundry about how the war should be pursued, the 40-year-old newly rejected First Lord of the Admiralty decided to enlist once again as a soldier and take his chance in the trenches.

Of course he couldn't resist a final letter of self-justification. 'Time will vindicate my adminstration of the Admiralty', he wrote to Asquith, 'and assign me my due share in the vast series of preparations and operations which have secured us the complete command of the seas.'

And then he was off to France. First he enlisted as a major in the Oxfordshire Hussars – on that first night (lest you should imagine he was actually slumming it) dining with the recently replaced C-in-C in France Sir John French and sleeping 'in a fine chateau, with hot baths, beds, champagne & all the conveniences'.

Next he was attached to the 2nd Batallion of the Grenadiers, whose colonel told him off-puttingly, 'I think I ought to tell you that we were not at all consulted in the matter of your coming to join us'.

Now he was indeed forced to muck in with the men, experiencing muddy dug-outs, rats and all the other components of life on the front line.

'It is satisfactory', he wrote home, 'to find that so many years of luxury have in no way impaired the tone of my system.'

But he nevertheless asked Clemmie to send him a large batch of necessities:

- A warm brown leather waistcoat
- A pair of trench wading boots, brown leather bottoms & waterproof canvas tops coming right up to the thigh
- A periscope (most important)
- A sheepskin sleeping bag
- 2 pairs of khaki trousers
- 1 pair of my brown buttoned boots
- three small face towels

His fellow guardsmen soon came to appreciate Churchill's down-to-earth manner, and he their professionalism, but he was eager for a command and kept agitating for it.

What he really wanted was a brigade – 'Do get a battalion now and a brigade later', Clemmie had advised him shrewdly – so he was less than pleased when the best they would offer him was indeed a humble batallion – the 6th Royal Scots Fusiliers, low in morale because most of its officers and half of its other ranks had recently been wiped out at the Battle of Loos.

Top gear

Churchill rather liked dressing up in any military uniform that was at all appropriate. In December 1915 he was taken on a tour of French positions, and their Tenth Army, then in front of Arras, gave him a bluish French steel helmet.

He consistently wore the helmet during the rest of his brief time in the trenches – a distinguishing feature rather like his cigars in more comfortable times.

He joined the battalion early in 1916, and (as with the Grenadiers) he wasn't initially given a warm welcome. After all, who was this toff to come in and give his orders to men who had suffered the full horrors of the trenches?

Here's what he brought with him this time:

- A black charger
- Two mounted grooms
- A vast array of luggage, including a long bath and a boiler for heating the bath water.

But things changed rapidly. Churchill was soon to lead his men back into the trenches, and by then they had come to respect him. He arranged sing-songs and football matches, smartened up their drill and exercised a firm but humane discipline. (A bit *too* humane, according to his commanding officer!)

There was no repeat of the Loos slaughter, but between 27 January and 6 March they were engaged in sporadic fighting during which he displayed his usual courage, including – it couldn't be otherwise – a few bold forays into no-man's land.

'I am fairly convinced that no more popular officer ever commanded troops', wrote his adjutant years later. 'He loved soldiering: it lay very near his heart and I think he could have been a very great soldier.'

Maybe – but it simply wasn't enough. The call of politics was too great.

Back in harness

Clemmie counselled against the wildness of it, because so many people thought he was a busted flush, but her restless husband was determined to make a mark in parliament all over again.

It took some time, and several speeches in drawing on his front-line experiences, but at last Lloyd George, now the Coalition prime minister, called him back into the Cabinet.

These were his next jobs:

- 1917 Minister of Munitions
- 1918 Secretary of State for War
- 1921 Colonial Secretary

These post-Gallipoli years saw him claw back a little of his reputation, but with his dynamic, cocksure approach he always made as many enemies as friends whichever job he was in.

Being in charge of munitions, for instance, wasn't grand enough work for him, so he spent as much time as possible near the action in France and getting in people's way.

Caterpillar tracks

While in charge of the nation's armaments during the war, Churchill naturally managed to vastly expand his ministry's budget. One new development he was particularly keen on was the 'tank', the brainwave of Ernest Swinton – then a lieutenant colonel and also, echoing Churchill, a war correspondent and the author of books (in his case fiction) with military themes.

The early versions of Swinton's baby were largely ineffective, being slow and cumbersome, but Churchill was of course right to recognise their potential – and in the Second World War a modern version would be named after Churchill.

When the war was over he skilfully managed the demobilisation of the army, but he made another nuisance of himself by trying to badger his colleagues into an aggressive stance against the Bolshevik regime in Russia – British and French troops could 'easily with the modern railways obtain control of Moscow' – at a time when they had had quite enough of war, thank you very much.

Winnie scrape 6

Despite being alarmed by his first experience in the air, Churchill soon decided it would be a good idea to learn to fly. He wasn't a natural, and after a few close calls Clemmie begged him to stop. He wouldn't listen.

One early evening in July 1919 he and an instructor took off from Croydon Aerodrome. With Churchill at the controls the plane immediately stalled, plunged to the ground and was badly damaged.

Clambering out with heavy bruises and scratches to his face, he nevertheless kept an appointment to preside at a House of Commons dinner. But this time he never took the controls again.

As Colonial Secretary, Churchill had an uprising nearer home to deal with: the Irish clamour for independence. In 1919 he had created the special constabulary force known as the Black and Tans, recruited largely from hardened soldiering men, to counter the Irish Republican Army. The resulting violence (on both sides) left a bad taste in many an Irish mouth.

Later he swung between two familiar Churchillian extremes. In 1922, when the IRA seized court buildings in Dublin, he was all in favour of the army shelling them with howitzers (the general in command affected to lack the necessary amunition), but soon afterwards he was happy to begin peace talks and went out of his way to wine and dine the IRA spokesman Michael Collins.

But everything was about to go wrong again. First he was admitted to hospital to have an inflamed appendix removed – then a fairly serious operation – and the very next day the government collapsed, necessitating a general election which he had every reason to fear.

Not so dandy

Churchill, newly out of hospital, wasn't in the best shape to conduct an election campaign – though he did, of course, from a distance, send a volley of manifestos to Dundee.

When he did arrive he found his audiences unresponsive, save for some angry heckling. He also got into an unwise spat with the local newspaper proprietor, D. C. Thomson, best known among children for his *Dandy* and *Beano* comics but in his own area for the morning *Dundee Advertiser*, the evening *Dundee Courier* and (also reaching further south) the *Sunday Post*.

Although one Dundee paper supported the Liberals and the other the Conservatives, both made vicious attacks on Churchill, for whom Thomson had developed a fierce dislike.

Rising to the bait, Churchill described his persecutor as 'a narrow, bitter, unreasonable being eaten up with his own conceit, consumed with his own petty arrogance, and pursued from day to day and from year to year with an

POLITICAL MAVERICK

unrelenting bee in his bonnet'. Thomson, for his part, noted that the campaigning Churchill was 'in a vile temper'.

The dogged prohibitionist

It's high time we met the wonderfully named Edwin Scrymgeour. Churchill first met him when he contested his Dundee seat back in 1908. He was running, hopelessly, as a scourge of the demon drink and took little more than two per cent of the vote.

But Scrymgeour wouldn't go away. In the two general elections of 1910 he polled first 15 per cent of Churchill's vote and then 20 per cent. In the by-election of 1917 he was still plugging away, and won 2,036 votes to Churchill's 7,302 – about 35 per cent – while in the general election a year later, though he still followed in the great man's wake, he managed to garner more than 10,000 votes.

Now his hour had come. Scrymgeour romped home in first place with a full 32,000 votes, while his old adversary came fourth and was out of parliament.

99

The hard-drinking working men of Dundee, it was said, had poured out of their locals in order to elect a temperance candidate – and Scrymgeour would go on to represent the town until 1931.

Churchill had a more glorious future ahead of him, but at this moment was ruefully glum: 'In the twinkling of an eye I found myself without an office, without a seat, without a party and without an appendix.'

Grief on grief

Detective Inspector Walter H. Thompson, for many years his bodyguard, later wrote a memoir in which he revealed that the reversal in Dundee threw Churchill into the greatest Black Dog despair he witnessed in all the time he worked alongside him.

But this dejection surely had deeper roots, his public fall from grace meshing with acute private loss. His mother had died in June 1921, and only three months later the Churchills lost their two-year-old daughter, Marigold, to a blood infection.

Two skips and a jump

Churchill declared himself to be without a party because he had been moving steadily to the political right and felt that his days with the Liberals were over.

They weren't quite, but another rapid round of elections went like this:

- 1923 For reasons none of his friends could understand he decided to stand for the Liberals at Leicester in the general election – and was soundly defeated.

- 1924 A by-election this time, and a shift from the Liberals but not quite to the Tories. He stood in Westminster as an Independent Anti-Socialist – and lost again.

- 1924 still, and another general election. This time he wore Conservative colours as he had last done 20 years before – and he won the Epping seat in Essex which (later renamed Woodford) he would hold for the rest of his parliamentary life.

Striking behaviour

Churchill was surprised and delighted to be given the no. 2 position in government, Chancellor of the Exchequer, in Stanley Baldwin's new Conservative cabinet.

But of course he hadn't the slightest doubt about his ability to do the job, and he was very soon unleashing all sorts of plans which rattled the cages of other ministers.

All that glitters

As Chancellor in 1925, Churchill returned Britain to the gold standard (that is, linked its currency to the price of gold), a move regarded by the economist John Maynard Keynes as foolish at a time when the country was still economically weak after the ravages of the First World War.

In 1920 he had published his book *The Economic Consequences of the Peace*. Now he brought out a pamphlet, under the Hogarth Press imprint of Virginia Woolf and her husband Leonard, entitled *The Economic Consequences of Mr Churchill*.

If this was typical Winston, even more so was the vigour he brought to dealing with the industrial strife which broke out in 1925 and resulted in the nine-day General Strike in the May of the following year.

It could be said, if a bit unkindly, that he'd brought it on himself. In returning sterling to the gold standard he threatened the prosperity of the coal mines, whose owners, in turn, threatened to close them unless miners took a severe pay cut. Not surprisingly the miners baulked at that: 'Not a penny off the pay, not a minute on the day' was their union's motto.

When more than a million of them were locked out of the mines some 1.7 million workers throughout the country came out on strike in sympathy with them.

It was a stroke of luck for Churchill that Baldwin – physically and mentally exhausted at the time – was happy to let his chancellor deal with the problem. After all, there was nothing Churchill liked better than handling a crisis.

He dealt with it in familiar fashion.
Churchill actually had little time for the
mine owners, who he thought grasping, and
he had a genuine respect for men who toiled
underground for poverty wages.*

Once attempts at compromise had failed,
however, he was hell bent on taking as many
over-the-top measures as might be necessary
in order to suppress the strike in what he
believed was the national interest.

With dockers having walked out, armed
soldiers accompanied convoys of food down
the East India Dock Road, and if Churchill
had had his way there would have been
tanks in the parade, too, with machine guns
placed at strategic positions along the route.

Baldwin at least prevented that, with one of
his advisers telling him that their hyped-up
chancellor 'thinks he is Napoleon'.

---

* Even George V, that arch enemy of socialism, replied to criticism
of the miners by saying 'Try living on their wages before you
judge them'.

The would-be general was also a would-be newspaper editor. Printers at the *Daily Mail* prevented publication of an editorial condemning the strike, but Churchill had the answer to that. He established the *British Gazette,* which ran for the duration of the conflict and gave the government's side of the argument.

Into the sunset

That was to be Churchill's last experience of high-level 'Action Man' politics for many years. He carried on as chancellor until the 1929 general election, when the Tories were ousted from power by Labour, and was then cast adrift – still a Member of Parliament, but one without the kind of major role he always coveted.

Life still held pleasures and challenges for him and yet, still in his mid-fifties, he must have wondered all through the next decade whether his sense of destiny was anything but a vainglorious dream.

These were to be known as the wilderness years . . .

❝No client that I have ever had, considering his well-filled life, has ever spent more time, trouble or interest in the making of his home.❞

CHAPTER four

HOME, SWEET CHARTWELL

I n the autumn of 1922, without telling Clemmie what he was up to, Churchill bought a brick-built farmhouse and 80 acres of land in the Kent countryside which they couldn't really afford.

She was horrified, but as usual threw herself into indulging her insufferably demanding husband, and Chartwell was to be their home for 40 years. Here, in a kind of modern Camelot, they would entertain a glittering array of the famous and the influential.

Here, too, Churchill was free not only to work, but to relax and play.

Dating of the timbers in the oldest part of the house shows that it was built during the reign of Henry VIII, but many changes had been made to it over the years, particularly during the middle of the 19th century. It wasn't an imposing building; it hadn't been lived in for a long while and it needed a complete overhaul.

The Churchills brought in the 'society' architect Philip Tilden to do the work. He had made a name for himself converting awkward old country houses into fashionable piles for the rich, and he was currently fashioning a completely new one for Lloyd George not very far away in Surrey.

Tilden found Chartwell an interesting challenge. Its walls were damp, the bricks running with moisture and home to spreading fungi, the timbers attacked by dry rot. He found Churchill an interesting challenge, too. After only a month he was having to explain to his client that he shouldn't expect to receive his plans for the renovation overnight: 'It takes a very considerable amount of time and thought', he wrote 'to produce things that matter so much.'

When he did get going on it, here are a few of the things he introduced:

- A completely new central wing at right angles to the rest of the house. (Churchill promptly christened it 'my promontory'.)
- A new kitchen and pantry.
- Five baths and fourteen lavatories. (Water piped in from outside was supplemented by a hydraulic ram in the grounds.)
- Telephones to keep Churchill in constant touch with the outside world.

While Clemmie looked after the interior decor, Winston had a hand in just about everything else. A later comment by Tilden can be interpreted either as a compliment or professional exasperation: 'No client that I have ever had, considering his well-filled life, has ever spent more time, trouble or interest in the making of his home.'

There was certainly some bad blood between them as the work dragged on and on – and as the cost of the enterprise rose from an original estimate of £7,000 to (a small fortune in those days) more than £18,000.

Chartwell today

To mark the 50th anniversary of the house being given to the National Trust, the Churchill's Chartwell appeal was launched in 2016 to raise £7.1 million and 'reinvigorate Winston Churchill's legacy'. The National Lottery Fund immediately made a grant of almost half this amount.

The house and grounds are very much as the Churchills left them because Lady Churchill's generosity ensured that most of the contents of the house and many of the couple's own possessions remained there. The anniversary appeal was designed to enable the purchase of hundreds of precious additional items already on display as loans (letters, books, medallions, uniforms, furniture and much more); to improve the interpretation of the great man's legacy; and to open rooms never seen by the public before.

• *Chartwell (National Trust) was designated a World Heritage Site in 1975. It's open every day except Christmas Eve and Christmas Day, with timed tickets for the house. Address: Mapleton Road, Westerham, Kent TN16 1PS. Telephone 01732 868381.*

Chartwell

1. Chartwell House
2. Lady Churchill's Rose Garden
3. Golden Orfe Pond
4. Swimming Pool
5. Swan Pen
6. Lake and island
7. Marlborough Pavilion

It was two years before the place was habitable, and it was the irrepressible Churchill who got in first: 'I am in bed in your bedroom', he wrote to Clemmie, '(wh I have annexed temporarily) & wh is sparsely but comfortably furnished with the pick of yr two van loads.'

Apprentice brickie

It was the view south across a valley to the Weald and Ashdown Forest that particularly appealed to Churchill. A local firm of landscape gardeners hoped to get in on the act, but they stood no chance: he much preferred to do things himself.

Chartwell was puny compared with the Blenheim in which he'd been born, but he perhaps had in mind Capability Brown's landscaping there when turning a humble pond into a second lake (he introduced black swans to it) by damming a stream. He enjoyed getting his hands dirty – 'wallowing in the most filthy black mud you ever saw, with the vilest odour' he wrote proudly to Stanley Baldwin.

He also loved building walls. A plaque proclaims that he was responsible for most of the brickwork surrounding the kitchen garden, and his other handiwork included a little hideaway (Marycot) for his youngest child, Mary.

No collection of Chartwell photographs is complete without one showing Churchill with a trowel in his hand. Unlikely as it may seem, he was also a card-carrying trade unionist: he delighted in being a member of the Amalgamated Union of Bricklayers.

Wordsmithing

The considerable expense of running Chartwell (eight or nine servants, three gardeners, a chauffeur, a groom and a bailiff, let alone the architect's fees and the cost of the renovation work) had to be met from the labours of Churchill's busy pen.

We've seen what prodigious amounts of writing he had already combined with a busy military and political life. Once out of office his output became almost demonic.

'A delightful month – building a cottage and dictating a book: 200 bricks and 2,000 words per day.'

There were, of course, costs involved here, too. He employed secretaries to whom he would dictate notes, letters, speeches and passages for his books at any time of the day or night that suited him – and whether he was on his feet, up on a ladder, tucked up in bed or wallowing in a bath.

He also relied on paid researchers to ferret out the detailed information he needed. His was the inspiration, and his were the words that spilled out with a rolling eloquence onto the page (he described the English sentence as 'a noble thing'), but the time-consuming donkey work had to be done by others.

A prime example of his fecundity is his five-volume account of the First World War, *The World Crisis*. The first instalment came out in 1923 and the whole thing was finished and in the bookshops by 1931 despite everything else he was involved in at the same time.

Along the shelves

It's been calculated that Churchill wrote more words than Shakespeare and Dickens combined. Here's a small selection of his books:

The story of the Malakand Field Force (1898)

The River War (1899)

London to Ladysmith (via Pretoria) (1900)

Ian Hamilton's March (1900)

Lord Randolph Churchill (1906)

My African Journey (1908)

The World Crisis (1923–1931)

My Early Life (1930)

Marlborough: His Life and Times (1933–1938)

Great Contemporaries (1937)

The Second World War (1948–1953)

A History of the English-Speaking Peoples (1956–1958)

He was careful to say that the work was 'not history, but a contribution to history'. Some of his critics agreed with him. When the first volume came out Bonar Law described it as 'autobiography disguised as a history of the universe', while an unnamed colleague quipped, 'Winston has written an enormous book about himself and called it *The World Crisis*'.

Down the drain

The chief literary enterprise of Churchill's 'wilderness years' was the biography of his ancestor John Churchill, the first Duke of Marlborough. With Chartwell making great demands on his finances, he might have used his healthy publisher's advance to pay off some of his debts or to settle an outstanding tax bill, but with typical brio he decided to invest the cash in the hope of making a quick killing.

The country on which he built his speculator's hopes was America, and the year was 1929.

Yes, you've got it – it was the year of the great stock-market crash.

In September 1929 Churchill was touring Canada and the USA to promote *The World Crisis* and writing to Clemmie about some 'extraordinary good fortune': a business friend had dealt shares for him at a handsome profit and, together with other forthcoming sources of income which he listed, 'there is money enough to make us comfortable & well-mounted in London this autumn'.

He now seemed affected by a rush of blood to the head. Over the next few weeks he invested wildly in oilfields, electricity ventures and gas companies in search of short-term profit – ignoring a telegram from his brokers which read, 'Market heavy. Liquidating becoming more urgent'.

By the end of October he was in despair. He claimed to have seen one of the fabled suicides leaping from a skyscraper as prices on the New York stock exchange collapsed, and he himself had, in today's terms, lost about half a million pounds overnight.

The family was so strapped for cash that Chartwell had to be closed and dust-sheeted.

But then, of course, he bounced back again. Ever the spendthrift, yet ever the cork that bobbed inexorably to the surface, he wrote furiously for the newspapers, completed more book deals and within a couple of years had more than doubled what he lost in the great crash.

Chartwell was reopened, and life returned to its extraordinary normal.

Winnie scrape 7

New York wasn't kind to Churchill during this period. In December 1931, while on another lecture tour, he tried to cross Fifth Avenue on foot and was hit by a passing car.

'Temperature 100.6', Clemmie wrote to their son, Randolph. 'Pulse normal. Head scalp wound severe. Two cracked ribs. Simple slight pleural irritation of right side. Generally much bruised. Progress satisfactory.'

Churchill admitted that the accident was his own fault – and the grateful driver both visited him in hospital and attended his next talk in Brooklyn.

A joy ride in a paint-box

Alongside his brick-laying and pond-digging, the restless man of action found relaxation in a pastime which would have surprised his younger self. Churchill discovered painting by accident in his early forties: in the low days after Gallipoli he came upon his brother Jack's wife Goonie in front of a canvas and was persuaded to have a go himself.

It quickly became an obsession, and – as with everything he touched – he didn't hesitate to enlist the help of experts. These included the artists Sir John Lavery and his wife Hazel, who were so encouraging that he immediately felt at home with a brush in his hand.

In his book *Painting as a Pastime* (yes, of course he wrote a book about it!) he described the sense of freedom the pair gave him: 'The canvas grinned in helplessness before me. The spell was broken. The sickly inhibitions rolled away. I seized the largest brush and fell upon my victim with Berserk fury. I have never felt any awe of a canvas since.'

He borrowed works from the collection of the connoisseur Sir Philip Sassoon so that he could copy them as learning practice; he worked shoulder to shoulder with William Nicholson (their treatments of the large lake at Chartwell sit side by side in the studio there); and he was coached in various techniques by the Camden Town artist Walter Sickert, who became a good friend.

Churchill took his brushes on his travels whenever he could, completed more than 500 paintings after that very first daub in 1915 – and was remarkably good at the craft.

- In 1919 his portrait of Sir John Lavery was accepted for the annual exhibition of the Royal Society of Portrait Painters in London.
- In 1921 the Galerie Druet in Paris displayed several of his paintings under the pseudonym Charles Morin, and six of them sold.
- In 1925 he entered his painting 'Winter Sunshine' anonymously at a London exhibition open to amateurs, winning first prize.
- In 1947 'Winter Sunshine' was accepted for the Royal Academy summer exhibition under the pseudonym David Winter.

'Happy are the painters', he wrote, 'for they shall not be lonely. Light and colour, peace and hope, will keep them company to the end, or almost to the end of the day.'

Today his canvasses fetch six- or seven-figure sums, *The Goldfish Pool at Chartwell* going under the hammer for £1.8 million, but he was modest about his talent. With no hope of matching the masters, 'we may content ourselves with a joy ride in a paint-box'.

feat of clay

Churchill might have mastered the plastic arts, too. The sculptor Oscar Nemon, whose bronze statue of Churchill stands in the Members' Lobby in the House of Commons, made several busts of him during the 1950s – one of them commissioned for Windsor Castle by the Queen.

On one occasion, despairing of his sitter's fidgeting, he gave him some clay to fashion while he worked. Churchill created a bust of Nemon (now on display at Chartwell) which the sculptor found astonishingly good for a complete beginner.

Animal pleasures

The house always had its resident dogs and cats,* and Churchill also delighted in stocking the grounds with colourful wildlife. Apart from the black swans with their vivid red bills, he introduced mandarin ducks to the lake and created ponds for golden orfe and other fish.

He developed a passion for butterflies, enlisting the help of the wildlife broadcaster L. Hugh Newman, who ran a butterfly farm just up the road from Chartwell. His dream was to have the garden aflutter with all kinds of exotic species, so he planted the thistles and buddleia they liked, had a running battle with the head gardener about nettles, and converted a summerhouse into a breeding station. He liked to sit inside it while the butterflies emerged from their chrysalides.

---

* At one time Churchill also had a pet budgie named Toby which he trained to carry a salt spoon and spill the contents on the dinner table. Toby was allowed to fly free, and apparently had a habit of dropping birdlime onto the bald pate of the Tory MP 'Rab' Butler.

Newman watched as Churchill put an arm into one of the cages, a British swallowtail alighting on his hand and 'pleasing him as much as if he had still been a boy'.

Churchill always did retain a childlike delight in simple things, and it's easy to imagine his pleasure when, shortly before a garden party at Chartwell, he released 600 peacock butterflies to enthrall his guests.

But what should we make of Churchill's suggestion that he might lay on 'fountains of honey and water' to attract thirsty butterflies? The eager lepidopterist Newman, appreciating that his client was both keen on inventions and an inveterate humorist, was unable to gauge whether he should take the idea seriously or not. (It never happened.)

Clemmie's contribution to the garden was more conventional, and can still be enjoyed today. She asked her cousin Venetia Montague to design her a formal rose garden, training roses and clematis up the walls and filling the beds with flowers such as lilies, fuchsias and ceanothus.

The old vegetable garden south of the house was no longer needed, as Churchill had enclosed a new one inside his skilfully erected brick walls, and here, as an avid tennis player, she had a new grass court laid out.

A warm dip

A favourite guest at Chartwell in the 1930s was the vegetarian, non-smoking, abstemious Frederick Lindemann, who held the chair of experimental philosophy at Oxford University. He was popular with Clemmie because he was the Swedish tennis champion and therefore added lustre to her new court, and with Winston because he provided the kind of intelligible scientific and technical information that Churchill could harness in developing his political ideas.

The Prof, as he was known, proved practically useful too. He was called on to assess the amount of water that would be needed for a new oval swimming pool at Chartwell, and to advise on ways of heating and cleaning it. Two coke-fired boilers were installed to maintain the water at 75°. The records show that parties were held there at all times of the year.

farmer Win

Being a gentleman farmer clearly appealed to Churchill. He had his horses, of course, but – as the Chartwell guidebook rather brutally puts it – his livestock 'tended either to die of disagreeable diseases or become fond pets'.

A branding iron on show in the house, with the letters WSC, reveals that he (briefly) owned a dairy herd, but it was his Middle White pigs that gave him the most pleasure – and sometimes pain, although as so often he managed to colour disagreeable personal news with a dash of humour.

'A minor catastrophe has occurred in the pig world', he wrote to Clemmie. 'Our best new sow, irritated by the noise of a pick-axe breaking the ground near the pig sty, killed six of a new litter of eight little pigs.

> 'Dogs look up to you, cats look down on you. Give me a pig! He looks you in the eye and treats you as an equal.'

'She was condemned to be fattened and to die, but today she has received the remaining two and proposes to bring them up in a sensible manner. She is therefore reprieved on probation.'

family tensions

It's glaringly obvious who got most out of the purchase of Chartwell. Churchill, frantically busy though he always was, never expected to lift a finger in keeping the show on the road – unless it was to click his fingers and see his staff come running.

He still travelled a lot, but a typical day at home went something like this:

- Have a sumptuous breakfast in bed at 7.30, sometimes even including roast beef.
- Stay in bed until 11, reading the papers and dictating notes and letters to a secretary.
- Take a bath at 11, stroll round the estate, and do a little work over a whisky and soda.
- From 1 o'clock preside over a long, three-course lunch, entertaining guests with brilliant monologues.

In defence of Napoleon

The strange case of the play *St Helena*, which opened at the Old Vic in London in February 1936, shows how Churchill couldn't resist meddling in things which were nothing to do with him – on this occasion to startling effect.

The play dealt with the last days of Napoleon, and early reviews were damning. Churchill, who clearly identified with the great leader, found time to attend a performance and then wrote a letter to *The Times* saying it was a 'an entertainment which throughout rivets the attention of the audience'.

R.C. Sheriff, its co-author, described its impact in his memoirs. On the night before Churchill's letter appeared there had been around 60 people in a theatre that could seat a thousand, whereas 'for the performance on the night following . . . more than five hundred people came, and on the next evening, the Saturday, the theatre was packed.

'Every seat sold, with people standing at the back of the pit and gallery. It must have been the most complete turnaround that had ever happened to a play before.'

- From 3 o'clock (or so) work, or paint, or lay bricks.
- At 5, take a siesta. (He picked up the 'power nap' habit in Cuba as a young man and claimed it allowed him to work 1½ days in every 24 hours.)
- Rise by 7, take another bath, dress for dinner.
- From 8 until late join the guests for a splendid spread followed by brandy and cigars.
- Midnight: into the study, glass in hand, for another work session, with a long-suffering secretary on hand to take more notes.

Out of office though he was for all these years, Churchill was unsparing in badgering political friends and enemies alike – always the knowing statesman-in-waiting with trenchant views on national and world events.

And now let's see it from Clemmie's point of view . . .

Although she, too, never had to lift a finger cooking the meals or making the beds, her grim role was to play second fiddle to a charismatic but infuriatingly selfish husband who (when he wasn't off doing exciting things with important people abroad) filled the house with guests she didn't much like.

These included the trio she thought of as 'The Terrible Bs':

Brendan Bracken
This young Irish acolyte and shameless chancer was a journalist, a banker and a Tory MP whose regular weekend visits to Chartwell became known as 'Bracken days'. The word got around, completely falsely, that he was Churchill's son – and Clemmie was very much not amused.

Lord Beaverbrook
Max Aitken, as he had been, was a Canadian businessman who was a millionaire by the age of 30 and who developed the *Daily Express* into the world's biggest-selling newspaper. Churchill, who agreed with him on Free Trade but not much else, called him his 'foul-weather friend' – and he would later put him to good use during the Second World War (*see page 154*).

Lord Birkenhead
F. E. Smith was a hard-drinking barrister, witty orator and former (Tory) Lord Chancellor. Clemmie didn't have to put up with him as long as the other two because he died in 1930 aged 58 from pneumonia brought on by cirrhosis of the liver.

And then there was Churchill's extravagance, of which Chartwell itself was the prime example. He would occasionally make vain attempts to curb his expenditure – 'No more champagne!' – but abstinence simply wasn't in his nature. To add to her insecurity, he couldn't resist dabbling in stocks and shares or gambling furiously in a casino.

It isn't surprising to learn that she would sometimes get very angry indeed. There's no doubt that they were genuinely a devoted couple (a letter from Clemmie in the early days of their relationship shows that it was a union built on desire: 'Je t'aime passionnément', she wrote, adding, 'I feel less shy in French'), but she was occasionally driven to rages and was even known to throw things at her impossible husband.

Kid gloves

How much time, in this febrile atmosphere, could they spare for their children? Very little, if truth be told. She was devoted to her husband's concerns – and so was he.

The Bali Dove

For a vibrant man of action Churchill was somewhat unusual in never attracting the slightest suspicion of infidelity. But did Clemmie ever stray? During the 1930s she was a guest, without Winston, on Lord Moyne's yacht the *Rosaura*, visiting a number of exotic islands, including Borneo, the Moluccas and the New Hebrides. On this trip it's said that she grew close to the wealthy art dealer Terence Philip, and some believe that the relationship developed into an affair.

It has to be said that nobody has ever come up with firm evidence to support this claim (and, indeed, many thought Philip gay), but Clemmie certainly looked back on that time with a special affection. She brought back from the holiday a Bali dove, and you can see its last resting place in the Chartwell grounds today. It lies beneath a large sundial and she had this poignant verse inscribed around its base:

> It does not do to wander
> Too far from sober men.
> But there's an island yonder,
> I think of it again.

'Father always came first, second and third', declared their youngest child Mary many years later. Her Woomany equivalent was her mother's first cousin*, whom she knew as Nana: 'She dominated my whole life when I was a child.'

The irony is that Churchill was well aware of how distant his own parents had been, yet was unable to avoid repeating the failing himself. Of course he loved his children dearly, and it was great fun when he pretended to be a gorilla and, beating his chest, chased the little ones around the garden. But they saw precious little of him.

In fact, so determined was Churchill that he shouldn't be the stern Victorian father that Lord Randolph had been that he lifted all restraints from the younger Randolph, who consquently appeared rudderless. All the children but Mary disappointed them.

---

* *Clemmie had learned a hard lesson. Poor little Marigold had been in the care of an inexperienced nanny when she fell ill. Clemmie, who was staying with aristocratic friends at the time, returned too late to save her.*

Before moving to Chartwell the family lived at a house called Lullenden, near East Grinstead in Sussex, and the neighbours were so alarmed by the feral behaviour of the Churchill children (then Diana, Randolph and Sarah: Mary was born soon after they moved into Chartwell) that they kept their own away from them.

Here's a chilling comment from Clemmie to Mary near the end of her life: 'I see you having such fun with your children, and I missed out on all that with mine.'

Over to you ...

Shortly before the birth of Marigold, their fourth child, in 1918, Clemmie offered to give her to her close friend Jean, Lady Hamilton. The Churchills were short of money at the time, while the Hamiltons had long since given up trying for a child of their own.

The proposed exchange only came to light many years later. In the event Marigold stayed with her parents throughout her brief life, and the Hamiltons eventually adopted two abandoned babies.

King and Country

As one year gave way to another at Chartwell it seemed that Churchill, for all his noisy self-promotion, had become a spent force in politics – a man whose moon had gloriously waxed and tragically waned. That feeling only intensified with his intervention in the abdication crisis of 1936.

It seems incredible today, but the national media had hidden from the people the intentions of their new king, Edward VIII, to marry the twice divorced American Wallis Simpson. (Their affair had begun on the very yacht, the *Rosaura*, on which Clemmie had enjoyed her Bali dove holiday.) When the news broke there was general outrage, and Baldwin's government very quickly came to the view that Edward couldn't both marry so tainted a woman – yes, of course, times have changed! – and remain on the throne.

Churchill's mistake was to totally misread the public mood. He had a one-to-one supper with the king, whom he counted a friend, and he believed he could help put things right.

'News from all fronts!' he wrote to Edward the following day. 'No pistol to be held at the King's head. No doubt that this request for time will be granted.'

He discovered how wrong he was when he stood up in parliament to defend him and was howled down by MPs from all sides. A few days later Edward abdicated.

Churchill's next speech, intended to put the best possible gloss on his behaviour, shows – certainly with hindsight – a further misjudgement of the monarch, asserting that 'his personality will not go down uncherished to future ages'.

He would very soon come to take a different view himself.

The old warmonger

Throughout the 1930s Churchill agitated for the build-up of British forces in response to German rearmament, and for many he was not only a voice crying in the wilderness, but a dangerous one.

By April 1939, when the future Tory prime minister Harold Macmillan visited Chartwell, that urgent voice was part of a growing chorus. The Italian dictator Benito Mussolini had just invaded Albania.

'It was a scene that gave me my first picture of Churchill at work', Macmillan wrote later. 'Maps were brought out; secretaries were marshalled; telephones becan to ring. "Where was the British fleet?"

'I shall always have a picture of that spring day and the sense of power and energy, the great flow of action, which came from Churchill, although he then held no public office. He alone seemed to be in command, when everyone else was dazed and hesitating.'

Macmillan perhaps sensed it: the fortunes of both the country and the man who had almost given up hope of ever leading it were about to change in the most testing, most dramatic fashion.

Churchill's hour had come . . .

'You ask, what is our aim? I can answer in one word: it is victory, victory at all costs, victory in spite of all terror, victory, however long and hard the road may be, for without victory there is no survival.'

CHAPTER FIVE

SAVIOUR OF THE NATION

hurchill's return to government and his elevation to the premiership at the grand old age of 65 came in two distinct phases less than two years apart.

First, at the outbreak of war, he was brought into Neville Chamberlain's cabinet in his former role as First Lord of the Admiralty. 'So it was', he wrote, 'that I came again to the room I had quitted in pain and sorrow almost exactly a quarter of a century before.'

The news was flashed around the Fleet by telegram: 'Winston is back!'

How the war began…

March 1938 Hitler's Germany annexes Austria (an event known as the Anschluss).

September 1938 The 'Munich Agreement' grants Hitler the Sudetenland area of Czechoslovakia inhabited mainly by German speakers.

March 1939 Germany occupies the whole of Czechoslovakia.

July 1939 Prime minister Neville Chamberlain commits Britain to supporting Poland if it is attacked by Germany.

September 1939 Germany invades Poland and Chamberlain announces, 'This country is at war with Germany.'

September 1939–May 1940 The 'Phoney War', with no major battles on the Western Front.

April 1940 The Germans invade Denmark and Norway.

10 May 1940 The 'Blitzkrieg' begins in France, Belgium, Luxemburg and the Netherlands, which are soon overrun.

He returned to the fray with his customary vigour, self-belief and imperiousness – fellow ministers, admirals and exhausted secretaries alike were kept on their toes from morning to night – and yet the major prize he had long sought still remained tantalisingly out of reach.

Let's not forget how unpopular Churchill had been within his own party. In November 1938 – less than a year before war broke out – he had faced de-selection by the Tories in his Epping seat, surviving by a vote of little more than two-to-one after a good deal of open hostility.

Why? Because when Chamberlain returned from Munich the previous month, hailing his deal with Hitler over Czechoslovakia as 'peace with honour', Churchill was foremost among those who condemned appeasement as abject and futile.

'The German dictator,' he told parliament, 'instead of snatching the victuals from the table, has been content to have them served to him course by course.'

Being proved right didn't immediately dim his reputation as leader of the awkward squad.

Here's the result of a public opinion poll taken in April 1940, when the war was going badly – the question being who should take over as prime minister if Chamberlain resigned:

Anthony Eden 28%
Winston Churchill 25%
Lord Halifax 7%
Clement Attlee 6%
David Lloyd George 5%

Tears and sweat

What weakened Chamberlain's position was a disastrously mismanaged attempt to drive the Germans out of Norway. Churchill, who had been blamed for Gallipoli, might have taken some of the rap for this debacle, too, but no mud stuck this time.

Instead he found himself one of the two front-runners for the premiership when Chamberlain stepped down in May.

Eden being ill, the other man in the frame was the foreign secretary, Lord Halifax, and many Tories preferred this traditional old-school leader to a character they regarded as a volatile, untrustworthy showman. Churchill wasn't King George VI's choice, either, but Halifax decided that a coalition government in wartime couldn't be run from the House of Lords, and he therefore stood aside. Churchill was ushered into 10 Downing Street.

When parliament assembled the following afternoon it was Chamberlain who was cheered to the rafters, while the new prime minister was given only a polite welcome from the Labour and Liberal benches.

This lukewarm introduction to what we now recognise as a momentous premiership was immediately transformed by one of the great Churchillian speeches that have echoed down the years:

'I would say to the House, as I said to those who have joined this government, that I have nothing to offer but blood, toil, tears and sweat...

'You ask, what is our policy? I will say: it is
to wage war, by sea, land and air, with all
our might and with all the strength that
God can give us: to wage war against a
monstrous tyranny, never surpassed in the
dark, lamentable catalogue of human crime.
That is our policy.

'You ask, what is our aim? I can answer in
one word: it is victory, victory at all costs,
victory in spite of all terror, victory, however
long and hard the road may be, for without
victory there is no survival.'

Dad's Army

It was Churchill who, reinstalled as First
Lord of the Admiralty, first put forward the
idea of a citizens' defence force to counter a
German invasion.

The trouble was that most of his colleagues
thought he was, in true Winston fashion,
exaggerating the risk – until, some eight
months later, Hitler's army was racing across
Europe and approaching the Channel coast.

Yes, he was right after all, and in May 1940 the secretary of state for war, Anthony Eden, announced the creation of the Local Defence Volunteers or LDV. He was hoping to recruit half a million men between the ages of 17 and 65 who weren't already in military service, and within two months he'd attracted three times that number. By 1943 the figure would rise to all of 1,750,000.

Things soon began to turn sour, though. Morale was low and discipline was poor. It wasn't just that this overwhelming response made it impossible to supply the volunteers with enough uniforms and weapons: there were fierce arguments about what they were actually supposed to be doing should the enemy arrive. Were they a passive unit, reporting to the regular army, or were they an active fighting force with their own command?

Enter Churchill again. Part of the morale problem, he decided, was the uninspiring name Eden had given his scratch corps. Out went the LDV and in came the new name of the Home Guard.

Out, too, went a million LDV armbands to be replaced by their Home Guard equivalents. Eden was furious about the cost of all this, but Churchill of course won the day.

from bad to worse

In later years, asked which period of his life he would choose to relive, Churchill replied, '1940 every time'. It was a simply dreadful year – but didn't he always flourish in adversity?

'I felt as if I were walking with destiny', he later wrote, 'and that all my past life had been but a preparation for this hour and for this trial.'

Here are a few of the 1940 horrors:

• In late May, as the German army drives with lightning force through western Europe, retreating British and other Allied troops are stranded on the beaches at Dunkirk. Some 338,000 of them are rescued by a motley flotilla of fishing smacks, pleasure boats and paddle steamers setting out from English ports.

• In June German forces occupy northern France, while 'independent' Vichy in the south elects a pro-German government. Britain and the Commonwealth now stand alone against Hitler.

• In July German U-boats begin attacking merchant ships in the Battle of the Atlantic, while the Luftwaffe, attempting to control the skies prior to an invasion, engages with the Royal Air Force over the south coast in the Battle of Britain.

• In September Germany launches the Blitz – murderous night-time bombing raids on London and other British cities.

Churchill never tried to deny the agonies people were suffering, and although he declared Dunkirk 'a miracle of deliverance' he refused to celebrate that incredible mass rescue as a triumph: 'Wars are not won by evacuations', he told parliament.

But he was brilliant at bolstering the never-say-die spirit of a nation whose fate hung in the balance. He toured the bombsites, visited the troops and the munitions factories and – perhaps his greatest contribution – stirred the millions tuned in to his 'wireless' broadcasts with magnificent, defiant oratory.

A way with words

In July 1940 the government wisely decided to scrap un-British plans to establish 'silent columns' – known as Cooper's Snoopers, after the name of the minister of information – to snitch on people guilty of spreading alarm and despondency in the wartime population.

Churchill, disarmingly admitting defeat, told parliament that the idea had 'passed into what is called in the United States innocuous desuetude'. *Smiles all round!*

After Dunkirk:

'Even though large tracts of Europe and many old and famous States have fallen or may fall into the grip of the Gestapo and all the odious apparatus of Nazi rule, we shall not flag or fail. We shall go on to the end...

We shall fight on the beaches, we shall fight on the landing grounds, we shall fight in the fields and in the streets, we shall fight in the hills. We shall never surrender.'

On the fall of France:

'Hitler knows that he will have to break us in this island or lose the war. If we can stand up to him, all Europe may be free, and the life of the world will move forward into broad, sunlit uplands; but if we fail, then the whole world, including the United States, and all that we have known and cared for, will sink into the abyss of a new dark age...

'Let us therefore brace ourselves to our duty and so bear ourselves that if the British Commonwealth and Empire lasts for a thousand years, men will still say, "This was their finest hour".'

After the Battle of Britain:

'Never in the field of human conflict was so much owed by so many to so few.' *

C'est la guerre

As a confirmed Francophile, who had always enjoyed holidaying (and painting) across the Channel, Churchill came to a grim decision when the defeated French agreed to deliver all their ships over to German or Italian control – their fleet, which had so recently been fighting alongside the British, posed a serious threat and would, unless it surrendered, have to be sunk.

---

* *His first version of the speech, rehearsed in his car on the way to parliament, read 'Never in the history of mankind...' But, his friend Pug Ismay asked, what about Jesus and his disciples? A grateful Churchill smiled – and changed it.*

Luckily much of the French navy was in British waters at the time, and only the crew of the giant submarine *Surcouf*, docked in Plymouth, put up a fight. One of them, plus a Briton, was killed in the skirmish. In the Mediterranean, however, there was a cluster of battleships, cruisers, destroyers and submarines at Oran, Algeria, and a smaller contingent at Alexandria.

'You are charged', read Churchill's message to the two admirals whose ships lay close by, 'with one of the most disagreeable and difficult tasks that a British admiral has ever been faced with, but we have complete confidence in you and rely on you to carry it out relentlessly.'

The French commanders were given four choices:

- To carry on fighting the enemy
- To sail to a British port
- To sail to a French port in the West Indies, where the ships would be demilitarised
- To scuttle their ships

The French commander at Alexandria came to terms, but Admiral Somerville at Gibraltar, though fresh from working alongside the French at Dunkirk, met a stony response from his opposite number at Oran.

At six o'clock the following evening, half an hour before an urgent Admiralty signal told him to get on with it, Somerville launched an attack which left 1,299 French sailors dead, 350 wounded, one battleship blown up, and another battleship and a cruiser beached.

In the Commons debate which followed, Churchill sat with tears running down his face as MPs accepted that he had done the right, if the callous, thing.

Ups and downs

Tears always came easily to Churchill, but so did a commanding brusqueness. The strain of keeping waverers on board during the dark early days of the war must have been immense – the Halifax faction was still counselling some kind of deal with Hitler – and reports on his behaviour vary wildly.

Some saw him as visibly ageing, depressed and prone to lose his concentration – and his eating and drinking habits can't have helped. His personal secretary reported his rations while spending a night deep underground during the Blitz: 'caviar (almost unobtainable in these days of restricted imports), Perrier Jouet 1928, 1865 brandy and excellent cigars.' He was growing steadily fatter.

Mean chow

Lord Woolton, the minister of food, advised the nation about eating healthily at a time of rationing, but a letter he received from Churchill made it clear that the great man wasn't in sympathy with a skimped regime:

'Almost all the food faddists I have ever known, nut-eaters and the like, have died young after a long period of senile decay. The British soldier is far more likely to be right than the scientists. All he cares about is beef.

'The way to lose the war is to try to force the British public into a diet of milk, oatmeal, potatoes etc, washed down on gala occasions with a little lime juice.'

He was also inclined to snappiness, as a frank letter from his 'loving devoted & watchful Clemmie' reveals:

My Darling,

I hope you will forgive me if I tell you something that I feel you ought to know.

One of the men in your entourage (a devoted friend) has been to me & told me that there is danger of your being generally disliked by your colleagues & subordinates because of your rough sarcastic & overbearing manner – It seems your Private Secretaries have agreed to behave like schoolboys & 'take what's coming to them' & then escape out of your presence shrugging their shoulders – Higher up, if an idea is suggested (say at a conference) you are supposed to be so contemptuous that presently no ideas – good or bad – will be forthcoming...

My Darling Winston – I must confess I have noticed a deterioration in your manner; & you are not so kind as you used to be.

It's unthinkable that he didn't take notice of this devastating warning – and in fact most of those who worked with and under Churchill spoke of him warmly in later days.

An infuriating loss

Churchill moved restlessly about the capital during the Blitz, so that his frustrated personal secretaries never knew in advance where they would be called in to work with him. One of them, John Peck, wrote a spoof minute which has survived:

Action This Day

Private Office

Pray let six new offices be fitted for my use, in Selfridge's, Lambeth Palace, Stanmore, Tooting Bec, the Palladium, and Mile End Road. I will inform you at 6 each evening at which office I shall dine, work and sleep. Accommodation will be required for Mrs Churchill, two shorthand writers, three secretaries and Nelson [his grey cat]. There should be shelter for all, and a place for me to watch air raids from the roof.

This should be completed by Monday. There is to be no hammering during office hours, that is between 7am and 3am.

W.S.C.

The mood swings are indisputable, but for every story about Churchill's supposed dodderiness there are several which show him in full command of a conference room or a supper table, waxing as lyrical and as incisive as few but he could manage.

No longer alone

As for the strain, that eased somewhat after two events which can now be seen as changing the course of the war.

Express production

With an eye for talent, Churchill appointed his friend and *Daily Express* proprietor Lord Beaverbrook as minister for aircraft production.

Crucially for 'The Few' in the Battle of Britain he built twice as many fighter planes as the Germans could manage. Launching his Harrogate Programme in January 1940, he aimed for the strangely precise supply of 3,602 planes a year – and actually achieved as many as 4,283.

- On 22 June, 1941, under the codename Operation Barbarossa, Hitler broke the German-Soviet Non-aggression Pact he had signed less than two years previously by sending a massive invasion force into the Soviet Union. Churchill distrusted Joseph Stalin and hated Communism, but Britain now had a new and powerful ally in the east.

The German army's initial progress was swift, but it would later become bogged down and then defeated at the Battle of Stalingrad (from August 1942 until February 1943), with the crippling loss of 150,000 lives.

- On the morning of 7 December, 1941, the Japanese Navy Air Service launched a surprise and devastating attack on the US naval base at Pearl Harbour in Hawaii – killing 2,403 Americans, wounding more than a thousand, damaging and sinking more than a dozen warships and destroying 188 aircraft.

Within days the USA had declared war not only on Japan, but also on Germany and Italy. Britain and the Commonwealth no longer stood alone.

Tobruk and after

Those who know Churchill only as a national hero will be surprised to hear the doubts that many had about him throughout the war.

In July 1940 he had boldly countermanded the views of his chiefs of staff by sending almost half the army's available tanks on a laborious journey round the Cape of Good Hope to reinforce British troops in the Middle East.

This would later come to be regarded as an astute move, but before eventual victory in that crucial theatre of war came the shock of Tobruk in June, 1942. Churchill received the news of what he called 'one of the heaviest blows I can recall during the war' directly from President Franklin D. Roosevelt while he was his guest in the White House.

The British garrison of 35,000 men had surrendered to a smaller German force. 'Defeat is one thing; disgrace is another', he would later say – and he began to fear that British soldiers were inferior to the enemy.

Back at home the finger was pointed at Churchill himself, and the following month he had to endure a two-day censure debate in parliament. A group of cross-party MPs had put forward a motion of 'no confidence in the central direction of the war' – an accusation directed at the prime minister as much as at the generals in the field.

A Windsor in the soup

Much as Churchill had liked the man who was briefly Edward VIII, he was ruthless in dealing with him once word got about that he had Nazi sympathies.

'I venture upon a word of serious counsel', he wrote to the Duke of Windsor in Lisbon. 'Many sharp and unfriendly ears will be pricked up to catch any suggestion that your Royal Highness takes a view about the war, or about the Germans, or about Hitlerism, which is different from that adopted by the British nation and parliament.

'I thought your Royal Highness would not mind these words of caution from your faithful and devoted servant ...'

Perhaps the most devastating attack came from the future Labour minister Aneurin Bevan, who declared scathingly, 'the Prime Minister wins debate after debate and loses battle after battle', adding, 'The country is beginning to say that he fights debates like a war and the war like a debate.'

The Tory MP Sir John Wardlaw-Milne thought he should stop meddling with army matters: 'The first vital mistake that we made in the war was to combine the offices of Prime Minister and Minister of Defence.'

Bletchley brains

Churchill was kept in daily touch with the boffins who broke the Germans' Enigma code at Bletchley Park. They read the enemy signals so successfully that around half the German U-boats were located and destroyed in the Atlantic.

Their vital work remained hush-hush, and after the war he described them proudly as 'My geese that laid the Golden Eggs and never cackled.'

It was lucky for Churchill that most of his detractors spoke far less well than he did, and that they had a scatter-gun approach to where the blame lay. He won this battle by a solid 477 votes to 27 – and although he must have felt bruised, he would fairly soon have reason to put the episode behind him.

In November General Montgomery (aka 'Monty') overcame Erwin Rommel's forces at El Alamein. Before Alamein, Churchill would later write, the Allies never had a victory, while afterwards they never suffered a defeat.

'This is not the end', he told parliament. 'It is not even the beginning of the end. But it is, perhaps, the end of the beginning.'

D~Day

When the beginning of the end eventually arrived two years later – Operation Overlord, in which the Allied forces landed on the Normany beaches in northern France to overthrow Hitler's army in Europe – Churchill was strangely reluctant to give the initiative his approval.

Bright ideas

Just as he encouraged the development of tanks in the First World War, so Churchill (with 'Prof' Lindemann as his adviser) gave inventors their head in the Second.

He created a specialist research department called Ministry of Defence 1, which became known colloquially as Winston Churchill's Toyshop and was charged with devising smart new weapons. It eventually had a staff of 250 men and women.

Oliver Lyttleton, minister of production in the wartime government, praised Churchill's 'eager readiness to listen to new, sometimes fantastic, ideas thrown up by scientists, engineers and academic figures'.

Artificial icebergs
This one sounds crazy, but it was seriously considered by the Combined Chiefs-of Staff in 1943. The eccentric Geoffrey Pyke created an extremely hard, slow-melting material (Pykrete) from ice and sawdust that could be moulded into artificial icebergs for Arctic waters and so serve as aircraft carriers. Allied success in the Battle of the Atlantic made the invention unnecessary.

Floating river mines
These little horrors, first promoted by Churchill at the Admiralty, were released in the Rhine and caused major disruption to shipping movements until the German occupation of eastern France made further discharges impossible.

Limpet mines
Attached by frogmen to ships' hulls, and held there by magnetic attraction, these were later detonated by a time-delayed fuse. More than a million of them were made – and they were responsible for sinking large numbers of enemy vessels.

Sticky bombs
Later named ST grenades, these were designed to be thrown at tanks and stick to them until they exploded. Having seen them tested, Churchill wrote a pithy memo: 'Make one million. WSC.'

The Great Panjandrum
One that never made it beyond a trial, this was very much the prime minister's baby – a massive wooden, rocket-propelled cart stuffed with explosives. The prototype careered all over the place during a demonstration, and Churchill had to make a dash to safety.

He at first opposed it partly because he thought the attack was in the wrong place – he argued for Operation Jupiter, which would have seen Allied troops land in Norway instead.

But it was also because, knowing the strength of Hitler's army, he feared that landing in France could be a bloody disaster. He thought of Dunkirk – and he no doubt remembered Gallipoli, too.

Dressing up

Churchill always grabbed the opportunity of putting on a uniform, but the abiding memory of his wartime wardrobe is the boiler suit. This became known as a siren suit, as it was an ideal garment to throw on at a moment's notice before hurrying off to a bomb shelter.

His portly figure and balding pate made him look a little like an overgrown baby, but of course he would settle only for the best. He had his siren suits made at the upper-class outfitters Turnbull & Asser – and fashioned from velvet.

'Unless there is a German collapse', he cabled President Roosevelt, 'the campaign of 1944 will be by far the most dangerous we have undertaken.'

The stark fact was that Britain was no longer top dog. When it came to making decisions, Churchill had to sit round the table with Roosevelt and 'Uncle Joe' Stalin, and they – representing greater powers – had rather more clout than he did.

When it came to Operation Overlord (yes, he lost the argument about Normandy), it was an American general, Dwight Eisenhower, who would be in charge, not a Brit.

As for Churchill himself, he was in poor health – his doctor had feared for his life during a fever in December 1943 – and he often seemed to lack his customary energy.

Nonetheless, by the following February he was writing to General George Marshall, chief-of-staff of the US Army, 'I am hardening very much on the operation as the time approaches.'

Leading from the front

And where did Winston Churchill hope to be on D-Day? Yes, you've guessed – in the thick of it on the beaches, with the bullets whistling about his head. 'What fun it would be to get there before Monty!' he chortled to his private secretary, John Colville.

Not only that, but he thought it would be a great idea to have the King alongside him. What a brave example that would be!

There were two reasons the generals thought this a stupid notion when they heard what he was planning.

1 He and the King stood a good chance of being killed, which wouldn't be great for morale.

2 Going by his past performances, he would be a wretched nuisance, interfering at every turn.

Fortunately George VI, having at first agreed to the wheeze, was leant on by his officials and realised that it wasn't such a good idea after all.

He wrote two letters to Churchill, asking him to call it off.

'Please consider my own position', he asked. 'I am a younger man than you, I am a sailor, & as King I am head of all three Services. There is nothing I would like better than to go to sea but I have agreed to stop at home; is it fair that you should then do exactly what I should have liked to do myself?'

The two Berlins

The garrulous Oxford philosopher Isaiah Berlin was employed as a government adviser in the USA during the war, sending home brilliantly entertaining dispatches, and Churchill relished the prospect of a stimulating exchange of views with him over a Downing Street lunch. It was a big disappointment therefore when his visitor seemed overawed, had little to say and replied to questions about the progress of the war with empty platitudes.

What Churchill discovered later was that there had been a ludicrous misunderstanding: the bewildered guest his aides had invited was the songwriter Irving Berlin.

This was the clincher, and Churchill reluctantly stayed at home – saying to Clemmie as they turned out the light on the night of 5 June, 'Do you realise that by the time you wake up in the morning twenty thousand men may have been killed?'

On a roll

He was six days behind Monty as it happened, paying a visit to the Normandy beachhead on 12 June. By then it was clear that Operation Overlord had been a great success, the Allies losing only 3,000 men on D-Day itself. The figure would rise to around 8,000 by the end of the month (two-thirds of them American), by which time the German army was on the back foot and Victory in Europe could be spied in the hazy distance.

Hitler now sent V1 rockets ('doodlebugs') over London, followed by the swifter, more deadly V2s. Churchill visited the bombsites in his usual way, but he was more often on his travels abroad for international talks in which he frequently clashed with Roosevelt and Stalin about how the war should be managed.

They were also beginning to discuss how eastern Europe should be carved up once the war was over, and that was another bone of contention. Churchill greeted 1945 by describing it as 'this new, disgusting year', but was in a jaunty mood later the same day, cabling Roosevelt with the stiffening message: 'No more let us falter! From Malta to Yalta! Let nobody alter.'

Meanwhile, back at home, the wartime coalition government which he had controlled and inspired so well in the dark days of the war was now in a mutinous mood. Churchill was no longer paying attention to detail. Clement Attlee, the Labour leader and deputy prime minister, typed (by his own hands) a scathing letter, describing what happened when committees met to discuss policy.

First they had to pass their minutes to two of the 'Terrible Bs' – the Lord Privy Seal (Beaverbrook) and the minister of information (Bracken) – who knew nothing of the facts but, as confidants of the prime minister, felt they had a right to air their ill-informed opinions.

What happened next was that Churchill turned up to meetings without having bothered to read his notes – and 'not infrequently a phrase catches your eye which gives rise to a disquisition on an interesting point only slightly connected with the subject matter'.

These difficulties both at home and abroad should have warned him that there had been a sea change, that whatever the greatness of his contribution to the war effort he might soon be yesterday's man.

And so it came to pass . . .

Another khaki election

Victory in Europe was declared on 8 May, 1945, and a general election was declared for 5 July.

The Labour and Conservative parties were each alloted ten political addresses on the wireless, and Churchill set the ball rolling on the first Monday of June. He made a disastrous mistake.

Friendly and respectful as he had been to his Labour colleagues in government, he ran a campaign which attempted to paint them as dangerous and subversive. Clemmie was among those begging him not to do it, but he wouldn't listen.

'They would have to fall back on some sort of Gestapo', he pronounced, 'no doubt very humanely directed in the first instance... My friends, I must tell you that a Socialist policy is abhorrent to the British ideas of freedom.'

What was it that the Labour Party intended to do?

- Create a National Health Service completely free for everyone who needed it.

- Begin a massive building programme to provide houses for families bombed out during the war or, because their menfolk (chiefly) had been fighting on soldiers' pay for years, had no other chance of finding somewhere to live.

- Nationalise the railways, coalmines and gas and electricity companies for the benefit of all.

For people who remembered the hungry 1930s when jobs were hard to find but the rich did very well for themselves, that programme sounded very appealing. And for men and women who had given some of the best years of their lives in the national cause on the battlefields and in the factories, it certainly didn't seem too much to ask.

Attlee, whom Churchill had sneeringly described as 'a modest man who has plenty to be modest about', used his own broadcast the following night to devastating effect.

'He wanted the electors to understand', Attlee said, 'how great was the difference between Winston Churchill, the great leader in war of a united nation, and Mr Churchill, the party leader of the Conservatives.

'He feared that those who had accepted his leadership in war might be tempted out of gratitude to follow him further. I thank him for having disillusioned them so thoroughly. The voice we heard last night was that of Mr Churchill, but the mind was that of Lord Beaverbrook.'

The verdict of the nation was as clear as a rifle shot – the 12 per cent swing to Labour in a landslide victory was (and remains) the largest ever recorded by any party in a British general election. Attlee had a majority of 145 seats.

Churchill, still leader of the Conservative Party, strode home with more than 70 per cent of the vote in his newly formed Woodford constituency – although it's worth noting that Labour and the Liberals had chosen not to oppose him, and an eccentric independent calling for a one-day working week managed to attract 10,000 votes.

'It only remains for me', he said in a dignified farewell speech, 'to express to the British people, for whom I have acted in these perilous years, my profound gratitude for the unflinching, unswerving support which they have given me during my task, and for the many expressions of kindness which they have shown towards their servant.'

And did he then fade gently into obscurity?
No – this was Winston Churchill . . .

‘the greatest
human being
ever to occupy
10 Downing Street’

CHAPTER SIX

TWILIGHT OF A GOD

hould Churchill, his chief life's work over and his Conservative policies overwhelmingly rejected by the British public, have stood down as leader of his party? Many of his own colleagues thought so – although none of them dared blurt it out to his face.

His own answer was 'No': if there was still a stage available to him, he fully intended to strut his stuff. And while most observers agreed he was a spent force, the man himself harboured notions of a political comeback.

Once again he was right!

First, though, there was time for a holiday. Off he went to Italy and France, and when he came back he had 15 completed canvases in his luggage. Stopping off at a casino in Monte Carlo he ran up a large gambling debt, but the manager kept his cheque as a souvenir rather than cashing it and so depleting his famous guest's rocky finances.

But things were about to look up on the economic front. Seventeen well-wishers, led by the *Daily Telegraph* owner Lord Camrose, raised about a million pounds in today's terms to buy Chartwell for the nation – presenting it to the National Trust on condition that the Churchills could live there until their deaths, after which it would become a shrine to the great man's achievements.

Meanwhile huge amounts of cash began to flow in from Churchill's latest literary enterprises. Having completed *The History of the English Speaking Peoples*, he now started his six-volume *The Second World War*, of which he said, 'This is not history; this is my case.' (History would judge him well, he would say to friends, because he would write it.)

His appearances in parliament were sporadic, despite his official leadership role, with his foreign secretary and next in line for the premiership, Anthony Eden, regularly deputising for him.

The Iron Curtain

Without the excitement of running a government, he turned to world affairs for his stimulation, making two major speeches in the year after the war ended, both of them abroad.

• At Fulton, Missouri, he made his famous Sinews of Peace speech, which warned of Russian aggression: 'From Stettin in the Baltic to Trieste in the Adriatic, an iron curtain has descended across the continent.' The Russians dated the Cold War from this moment, while many in the West weren't yet ready to listen. It was that old warmonger Winnie again!

• In Zurich he argued for a United Europe, combining 'a spiritually great France and a spiritually great Germany'. France wasn't yet ready for that idea!

Ticking over

Churchill spent a few years touring the globe and putting quite a few backs up with his radical solutions to a world in crisis. And then, miraculously, he found himself back in the saddle again . . .

At the 1950 general election Labour's majority was slashed to only six seats, and it soon became clear that an exhausted government couldn't cling on for long.

Turf wars

In 1949, at the age of 75, Churchill became a racehorse owner, encouraged by his son-in-law Christopher Soames. His first purchase was a grey, Colonist 11, which won 13 races from 24 starts, and he eventually owned 36 racehorses and a dozen brood mares.

The stable colours were those of his father, Lord Randolph, who had won the 1889 Oaks at Epsom with his black filly L'Abbesse de Jouane: pink, with chocolate sleeves and cap.

The following year there was another election. This time Labour had slightly more votes than the Tories – indeed, at 13.9 million it was the largest ever clocked up by a British party until the Blair government in 1997 – but the vagaries of the electoral system gave Churchill a small, but sustainable majority. The Conservatives would be in power for a further 13 years.

How was this regarded at Chartwell? We can only imagine the horror with which Clemmie envisaged the manic activity starting up all over again, especially since Churchill's health was steadily (sometimes alarmingly) deteriorating and his girth equally steadily expanding: Churchill demanded that she buy a new set of scales when the bulk perched on his small frame was shown to weigh all of 95 kg (15 stone).

As for the severe diet that she suggested: 'I have no grievance against a tomato, but I think one should eat other things as well.'

On top of that, he was deaf yet refused to wear a hearing aid. After all, he was the one doing the talking.

And how was Churchill's premiership regarded by the cabinet? With huge frustration. He wasn't only making a pig's ear of leading the government, but he was standing in their way: several of them had an eye to the top spot, but he made it very clear that he didn't intend to budge.

Eden, he commented, had 'hungry eyes'.

When he suffered a massive stroke in June, 1953 – moments after making a sparkling speech at a Downing Street dinner – they must have been sure that their time had come. He retired to Chartwell for a month, took to a wheelchair, found it impossible to shape his lips to take a cigar and was for a time a pathetic shadow of the wartime giant. 'Dazed and grey', according to his daughter Mary, he did indeed consider resigning.

But he was Churchill. He came bouncing back, simply indefatigable. Whenever he toyed with calling it a day some international summit or crisis demanded that he stay to help sort things out. His stroke hidden from the public, he couldn't face an inactive life.

> "I feel like an aeroplane at the end of its flight, in the dusk, with the petrol running out, in search of a safe landing."

'This simply can't go on', Eden is reported as saying. 'He is gaga – he can't finish his sentences.'

At last Churchill's colleagues forced the issue. Seven of them, including the future premiers Eden and Macmillan, swooped on him in an 'Et tu, Brute' moment – officially to discuss the date of the next general election, but in reality to topple him. It was, Macmillan wrote later, 'rather a painful occasion'. Churchill knew full well what they were up to. When he said it was clear they all wanted him out, not one of them offered a consoling reply.

On 5 April, 1955 the proud 80-year-old premier was driven to Buckingham Palace to tender his resignation to the young Queen Elizabeth. Although he would remain an MP for nearly 11 years, he would never make another of his memorable speeches in the House of Commons.

Grateful thanks

Churchill's last years were dogged by ill health, including further strokes, but his reputation was undimmed. Both before and after his resignation the honours poured in:

- The Nobel Prize for Literature
- Honorary citizenship of the United States
- The freedom of 40 British towns and cities
- Statues around the world, including the one by Ivor Roberts-Jones in Parliament Square
- Nine honorary degrees
- 37 orders and medals

To mark his 80th birthday the House of Commons commissioned a portrait by the celebrated artist Graham Sutherland. Clemmie described him to her daughter Mary as 'a wow' adding that 'he really is a most attractive man & one can hardly believe that the savage cruel designs which he exhibits come from his brush'.

When the work was finished, Churchill certainly found it cruel: it showed him as old, weak and grumpy.

'The portrait is a remarkable example of modern art', is the best he could find to say of it at the official unveiling. 'It certainly combines force and candour.'

In Oscar Wilde's novel *The Picture of Dorian Gray* a portrait kept in the attic visibly ages while the beautiful young man it depicts retains his youth and vigour in society. Alas, although Clemmie immediately consigned Sutherland's work to the Chartwell attic, there was no denying her husband's decline. A year or so later she cut it up and burned it.

Mourning cranes

Churchill died, aged 90, on the morning of Sunday January 24 – by a coincidence the 70th anniversary of Lord Randolph's death.

Such was his lustre that he was the only commoner apart from Nelson, the Duke of Wellington and William Gladstone to be given a grand state funeral. The service was in St Paul's Cathedral, the coffin later being carried by boat along the Thames and then by train to Bladon churchyard.

An unforgettable image of this procession was the lowering of riverside cranes in silent salute as the coffin passed down the Thames.

Let's leave the last word to Roy Jenkins, the author of massive biographies of Gladstone, who he counts the best prime minister of the 19th century and Churchill, who gets his vote for the 20th. He originally thought Gladstone the greater man, but came to change his mind the further his researches took him.

'I now put Churchill, with all his idiosyncracies, his indulgences, his occasional childishness, but also his genius, his tenacity and his persistent ability, right or wrong, successful or unsuccessful, to be larger than life, as the greatest human being ever to occupy 10 Downing Street.'

Glossary

Blitzkrieg Literally 'lightning war', a tactic of German forces to disorganise enemy forces, characterised by swift artillery attacks with close air support.

Boers Descendants of Dutch-speaking settlers in the Cape area of South Africa.

Bolsheviks Members of the Russian workers' party led by Lenin, which seized control of the country in 1917 and became the dominating power.

Camden Town artists English post-Impressionists who gathered in Walter Sickert's Camden Town studio.

Harrow Founded in 1572 and (with Eton) one of the two most famous independent boys' boarding schools in England.

Hussars Light cavalry regiments deployed principally in the 18th and 19th centuries.

Low Church A form of Christianity which dispenses with ritual and priests, its adherents instead experiencing a one-to-one relationship with God.

Mahdi, The A religious leader in Sudan who proclaimed himself the messianic redeemer of the Islamic faith and in 1885 seized Khartoum.

No-man's land The unoccupied (and dangerous) area between two entrenched opposing armies.

Stock-market crash 1929 On Black Tuesday thousands of investors were bankrupted as share prices collapsed. The Great Depression followed.

U-boat A German submarine (*Unterseeboot*).

Churchill Timeline

1874 Born (30 November) at Blenheim Palace.

1881 Is sent to St George's school in Ascot, where he is flogged.

1883 Enrols in a prep school in Hove; learns to ride.

1886 Enters Harrow.

1893 Joins the Royal Military Academy, Sandhurst, after passing the entrance exam at the third attempt.

1895 Visits Cuba and comes under fire on his 21st birthday; joins 4th Hussars cavalry; father Randolph dies.

1896 Sets sail for India and Afghanistan, where he both serves as a soldier and works as a journalist.

1898 Spends two months in the Sudan and takes part in the Battle of Omdurman.

1899 Leaves for South Africa as a journalist, but becomes involved in a Boer War skirmish, is arrested as a prisoner of war and makes a dramatic escape. Returns to England and becomes 'world famous overnight'.

1900 Enters parliament as Tory MP for Oldham.

1904 Joins Liberals over tariff reform.

1906 Wins Manchester North seat.

1908 Becomes president of Board of Trade at the age of 33; is voted out of his Manchester seat and finds another in Dundee; marries Clementine Hozier.

1910–11 Home secretary: miners' strike in the Rhondda and the shoot-out on Sidney Street.

1911 Is appointed First Lord of the Admiralty.

1915 Gallipoli disaster during the First World War; loses his job and serves in the trenches on the Western Front.

1916 Commands the 6th Royal Fusiliers.

1917 Rejoins government as minister of munitions.

1919 Becomes war and air secretary; creates the Black & Tans in Ireland; survives light aircraft crash at Croydon Aerodrome.

1921 Becomes colonial secretary; the Churchills' two-year-old daughter Marigold dies.

1922 Loses his seat in general election and is 'without a seat, without a party and without an appendix'. Buys Chartwell.

1923 Is defeated in another general election, standing for the Liberals in a Leicester seat.

1924 At a by-election stands in Westminster as an Independent Anti-Socialist and loses again. Switches to the Conservatives and wins in Epping. Becomes chancellor of the exchequer.

1925 Returns Britain to the gold standard.

1926 General Strike; establishes the *British Gazette* to present the government's position.

1929 Labour ousts the Tories in a general election and Churchill is out of government for ten years. He loses money in the US stock-market crash.

1931 Knocked down by a car in New York.

1936 Roundly condemned for his intervention in the Edward VIII abdication crisis.

1939 Outbreak of war: becomes First Lord of the Admiralty for the second time.

1940 Norwegian Campaign disaster; Chamberlain resigns and Churchill becomes prime minister for the first time at the age of 65; he makes a series of stirring speeches as Britain and the Commonwealth stand alone. Defeat in France is followed by the 'miracle of deliverance' at Dunkirk, the aerial Battle of Britain and the London Blitz.

1941 Hitler attacks the Soviet Union, and the Japanese assault on Pearl Harbour brings the Americans into the war.

Churchill Timeline

1942 Churchill survives a Commons censure debate after defeat at Tobruk, but this is followed by victory at the Battle of Alamein.

1944 On 6 June Operation Overlord sends some 156,000 Allied troops onto the Normandy beaches.

1945 After a landslide victory for Labour in the general election, Churchill remains leader of the Tories but is out of power again.

1946 At Fulton, Missouri, Churchill warns about the Russian Iron Curtain descending on Europe. Chartwell is bought for the nation by well-wishers and given to the National Trust, with the Churchills allowed to live in it until their deaths.

1950 Labour wins a much diminished majority in a general election.

1951 At another general election Labour wins most votes, but the Tories most seats. Churchill begins his second spell as prime minister.

1953 He suffers a massive stroke, which is hidden from the public, but makes a miraculous recovery and clings on to power.

1954 To mark his 80th birthday, parliament commissions a portrait by Graham Sutherland. Churchill hates it – and Clemmie later destroys it.

1955 After pressure from his cabinet colleagues he tenders his resignation to the Queen. He remains party leader for a time.

1964 He retires from political life.

1965 He dies (24 January) and is given a state funeral before being buried alongside his parents at the village church of Bladon, near Blenheim Palace.

Index

Cherished Library

Some other
Very Peculiar Histories™

The Blitz
David Arscott
ISBN: 978-1-907184-18-5

London
Jim Pipe
ISBN: 978-1-907184-26-0

Castles
Jacqueline Morley
ISBN: 978-1-907184-48-2

Make Do and Mend
Jacqueline Morley
ISBN: 978-1-910184-45-5

Charles Dickens
Fiona Macdonald
ISBN: 978-1-908177-15-5

Scotland
Fiona Macdonald

Golf
David Arscott
ISBN: 978-1-907184-75-8

Vol. 1: From ancient times
to Robert the Bruce
ISBN: 978-1-906370-91-6

Great Britons
Ian Graham
ISBN: 978-1-907184-59-8

Vol. 2: From the Stewarts
to modern Scotland
ISBN: 978-1-906714-79-6

Ireland
Jim Pipe
ISBN: 978-1-905638-98-7

Wales
Rupert Matthews
ISBN: 978-1-907184-19-2

Kings & Queens
Antony Mason
ISBN: 978-1-906714-77-2

Whisky
Fiona Macdonald
ISBN: 978-1-907184-76-5

Visit
www.salariya.com
for our online catalogue and
free fun stuff.